PRAISE FOR GANGA STONE'S
START THE CONVERSATION

P9-DWC-762

GANGA STONE

START

the

CONVERSATION

THE BOOK ABOUT
DEATH YOU WERE
HOPING TO FIND

A Time Warner Company

Copyright © 1996 by Ganga Stone
All rights reserved.

Warner Books, Inc., 1271 Avenue of the Americas, New York, NY 10020
Visit our Web site at
http://pathfinder.com/twep

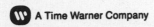 A Time Warner Company

Printed in the United States of America
First Trade Printing: June 1997
10 9 8 7 6 5 4 3 2 1

Library of Congress Cataloging-in-Publication Data
Stone, Ganga.
    Start the converstion : the book about death you were hoping to find /
Ganga Stone.
      p.   cm.
    ISBN 0-446-67280-7
      1. Terminally ill—Religious life. 2. Death—Religious aspects.
3. Consolation. 4. Stone, Ganga.   I. Title.
BL625.9.S53S73 1996
291.2'3—dc20
                                  95-25569
                                       CIP

Book design by Barbara Balch

THIS BOOK IS DEDICATED to all who are grief-stricken at this moment and to all who are approaching their own death with fear. May your anguish be eased, may it be erased by the ideas in this book.

May you have the grace to trust what you find here and the courage to apply these simple teachings in your own life right now. May peace and confidence replace your grief and your fear. May the truth comfort you as only the truth can: There is no death.

This work is dedicated as well to Dr. Elisabeth Kübler-Ross. Elisabeth began, over a quarter of a century ago, to speak out about the isolation and abandonment suffered by dying people in our hospitals and, indeed, everywhere. All the work being done in the now-familiar field of Death and Dying owes its existence to her. She alone broke the ground. In solitude she plowed it and seeded it. And the harvest is immense. It is hard even to imagine that such a short time ago there were no books on the shelf, no hospices in the very next town, no support groups, no conversations about death at all.

Anyone who plans to be dying owes a tremendous debt to Elisabeth. We are too near the base of the mountain to measure its height. The scope of her contribution will be clearer when another quarter century has passed. From where I sit, it looks very very important. Carry on, Elisabeth. May the fruit of your life's work bring you joy.

ACKNOWLEDGMENTS

I OWE SO MUCH to the efforts of those dying friends whose willingness to apply this new approach to their own death made it possible for me to assure you that this method *has* been tested by human beings, and it works. It will work for you, too.

For challenging me with good questions and plenty of them, my thanks go to Donald Adler, Stu Colby and the late great Tomato Bob. Also thanks to everyone who came to class, especially during the early years when the work was still taking shape. Kay Mitchell kept me steady just by being there. Judy Loza continues to make it so easy to teach. Thanks for all your time, both of you.

As a person whose relationship to earning a living has always been a bit spotty, I am forever grateful for the ongoing kindness of a bouquet of benefactors. It was they who jumped in when necessary, who kept my feet shod, if not on the ground, my belly full, and a roof over my highly impractical head. The most sustained and significant of these life preservers was Constantine Photopoulos.

Costa appeared in my life ten years ago. I was making a marginal living selling coffee and croissants on the street, and focusing on volunteering at Cabrini Hospice the rest of the time. I believed I had something to share with dying people, and I was sure I had a lot to learn from them. Costa retired me from street vending to work full time for God's Love We Deliver, the meal program for homebound people with AIDS that had grown out of my hospice volunteer work.

Hungry people cannot take much interest in any conversation, however comforting it may be. The meal program had to come first. Costa gave a newborn God's Love We Deliver its initial rent, phone and postage money. And he supported the start-up of my daughter's life, too, by making sure I had all I could eat throughout the pregnancy. I ate a lot. After Hedley arrived, Costa offered her both time and tenderness, which gave me the chance to develop this book. I know God sent him to us, but Costa was always free to decline the assignment. He made everything possible. God knows.

Aunt Lil's generous 1985 bequest allowed me to pay attention to big questions like "what is death?" rather than little ones like "where is the rent?" I jokingly called it the Lillian Stein Career Development Award, because what sort of career was being developed wasn't all that clear. Aunt Mary discharged her administrative duties with great patience and care. She never was properly thanked, until now. Thanks, Mary. You too, Auntie Elsa, for everything.

So many wonderful people have helped along the path, in large ways and small. Every single gesture of encouragement and support is remembered and always will be. I cannot name you all here, but you know who you are. Betsy Carter, here's to you. Miss Jane Best, too.

CONTENTS

Foreword: Benjamin Franklin on Death xi

Preface xiii

Introduction 1

CHAPTER ONE: IT'S NOT FAIR 9

CHAPTER TWO: THE ANNIHILATION PREMISE: FEAR AND GRIEF 21

CHAPTER THREE: WHAT IS PROOF? 27

CHAPTER FOUR: MAKING SENSE OF THE NEAR-DEATH EXPERIENCE 31

CHAPTER FIVE: THE SURVIVOR JOURNEYS ON 49

CHAPTER SIX: THE SURVIVOR HERE AND NOW 57

CHAPTER SEVEN: THEN WHAT DIES? AND HOW DOES IT DIE? AND DOES DYING HAVE TO HURT? 85

CHAPTER EIGHT: REVISITING FEAR AND GRIEF 105

CHAPTER NINE: HOW TO PREPARE: REGRET-PROOFING YOUR LIFE 151

CHAPTER TEN: DEALING WITH DYING 165

A Note to Clergy 181

FOREWORD

Benjamin Franklin on Death

I CONDOLE WITH YOU. We have lost a most dear and valuable relation. But it is the will of God and nature that
these mortal bodies be laid aside when the soul is to
enter into real life. This is rather an embryo state, a preparation for living. A man is not completely born until he be
dead. Why then should we grieve that a new child is born
among the immortals, a new member added to their happy
society.

We are spirits. That bodies should be lent us, while they
can afford us pleasure, assist us in acquiring knowledge, or
in doing good to our fellow creatures, is a kind and benevolent act of God. When they become unfit for these purposes, and afford us pain instead of pleasure, instead of an
aid become an encumbrance, and answer none of the inten-
tions for which they were given, it is equally kind and
benevolent that a way is provided by which we may get rid
of them. Death is that way.

We ourselves, in some cases, prudently choose a partial
death. A mangled painful limb which cannot be restored we
willingly cut off. He who plucks out a tooth parts with it
freely, since the pain goes with it, and he who quits the
whole body, parts at once with all pains and possibilities of

pains and diseases which it was liable to or capable of making him suffer.

Our friend and we are invited abroad on a party of pleasure which is to last forever. His chair was ready first, and he is gone before us. We could not all conveniently start together; and why should you and I be grieved at this, since we are soon to follow, and know where to find him?

PREFACE

I T WAS 1964. I was not quite twenty-three and living on my own in St. Louis. In the fall of that year, I made the trip back to New York for a family reunion of sorts. My dad had been away at sea on the SS *Hope* for ten months. Now, in mid-September, he was due back.

My parents' marriage was not without its problems, but it seemed in this, its twenty-fifth year, likely to last. The physical complaints my mother had been issuing during her husband's absence—weakness in her fingers and legs, loss of energy, fatigue—were probably a function of loneliness. That was my assumption, bolstered in mid-July by her report that the numerous tests she had been hospitalized for had shown no disturbing results.

So it was with amazement that I saw, as she came toward me on the pier, that she was scarcely able to walk. Her gait was uncertain, uncoordinated and strange. She was wobbly as a brand-new colt.

We didn't speak of it, but went home with my father as if nothing were wrong.

The next day my dad saw her doctor, the same doctor who had assured us that there was no problem, and that's when we learned she had ALS—Lou Gehrig's disease—

(though for me it will always be Winifred Stone's disease) and would be dead in less than a year.

I remember just where I stood when he told me. I was in my sister's room alone. My dad walked in without knocking and said, "Your mother will be dead in under a year," and walked out.

I remember the trapdoor that dropped open beneath my feet. I remember the terrifying free fall into space. I remember the horror that swallowed me up. I remember the grief that seized my spirit, that stole my joy, that wouldn't ever let go.

I remember the strained efforts to "act normal" around my mom. I remember the isolation each of us drew into, as no mention could be made of the only thing we all shared.

I spent some days at home and then flew back to St. Louis. But now I couldn't concentrate on my work: my mind wandered, my hands shook. My boss Sarah was a neuropathologist. She told me that my mother's disease was rare. Therefore, Sarah matter-of-factly said, she'd be grateful to get some tissue, either at autopsy or before. I remember thinking, *But it's my mother . . . it's my mom.*

Nowhere in my excellent private school education and at no time in the years of college that followed had anyone ever mentioned this possibility—"Hey, you know, your mother might die." Perhaps, just perhaps, the shock would have been less profound had it dawned on me, just once, that this might be.

As it was, there were no tools whatsoever in my kit. Our upbringing had been "ethical-humanist," for want of a better term. We were activists, politically aware and involved people whose idea of good rested in social change. There was an atmosphere of superiority to and some contempt for matters religious or spiritual, though my mother did harbor an ill-concealed longing to find some way back to the Lutheran faith of her youth. The closest she came was an off-again, on-again relationship with a local Unitarian church. My father barely tolerated it and we kids never understood why she bothered.

So there I was—there we all were, really—without a clue, without an ally, without hope.

In the months following her diagnosis I began a series of rather crazed solo drives between St. Louis and Baltimore. I could not sit still in St. Louis—the pain was too great. Nor could I come back to New York—that would alert her (as if she didn't already know it) that something was wrong. And so I drove my long '57 Plymouth, red with white fins, making trip after trip—my stash of cigarettes and No-Doz beside me on the seat.

From Baltimore, where my boyfriend was in school and a waitressing job was easy to get, I'd make little weekend forays to New York, dropping in as if casually on my mother—noting with horror the weakness taking over her big, once-robust frame.

Finally, in January, she fell on the way to work and couldn't get up again. She quit her job then and began to be at home in bed. Because it was now official and obvious, I could move back to New York. And so in the first months of the new year, I did.

She stuck it out for seven months more. I visited every day. We never said that she was dying—never said a word. My mother was an intelligent woman, a librarian. She had surely done the research. No doubt she knew the name of what she had. But we never spoke of it.

A minister from her hometown in Wisconsin tried to see her. She refused. A favorite niece came to visit from California. She stayed three weeks. They talked and talked. Right after Carol left, my mother said, "That's it, it's time to go to the hospital." She couldn't speak after that, or move her body. Not being able to turn the pages of book, not being able to read or converse—these were not acceptable conditions of life for my mother. "Let's go," she said.

It was a Thursday evening—July 15, 1965—around 5:30. We took her down to the ambulance in a wheelchair, knowing she was leaving her home for the last time. Some neighbors paused to say good-bye on the quiet street in front of our building, warily but tenderly stroking her powerless hands. There were tears.

There was no bed available at the hospital, so they set one up in the visitors' lounge. I stayed there with her, sleeping on the sticky vinyl couch beside her bed. The doctor went out of town for the weekend right after he admitted her.

I remember the hours I spent, pockets heavy with change, sweating and crying in the phone booth in that visitors' lounge. I was frantic, desperate, suffocating in almost unspeakable pain, talking to anyone I could get. How could this possibly be? How? I had no way to contain my agony. I thought I would explode.

At last, on Monday, there was a meeting with her doctor. My sister and I agreed beforehand to support our father in instructing the doctor not to try any extraordinary measures to sustain her life. We asked when she might die. He said it could be days—or weeks. My father and sister went home. I caught up with the doctor in the hall.

"Look," I said, "this can't go on. I want you to up her codeine from 15 mg to 45."

"That would suppress her respiration," he said.

"That," I said, "is what I want."

I watched him write the order in the chart. The next shot

was scheduled for two o'clock. My mother had her own nurse now, who was on her lunch break at two. I went and got her. I made sure she saw the change in dose. I watched her give the shot.

The nurse sat knitting. I held my mother's hand. "Don't worry, Mommy, this won't be hard. I'm right here with you, don't be afraid." By 2:30 my mother's hand was cooling, her breathing getting slow. I kept talking calmly, though a mounting panic held my heart. Everything seemed to move so slowly. It was all so surreal. The bluish color crept up her arm as I watched fascinated, horrified.

At 3:10 a tear, just one, slid down my mother's cheek—the one nearest me, the left cheek—her head tipped slowly back—how?—her mouth dropped open—and she was gone.

I could see that what remained on the bed was no longer my mother. It was some *thing,* not some *one,* though it was years before I understood the implications of that distinction.

Interns came running in, leapt up on the bed and began to pound at her chest with their big fists. "Stop it, stop it!" I screamed. "Leave her alone . . . leave her alone . . . leave her alone!"

Orderlies came to take the vacated body away. But first they returned all the other patients to their rooms, in order, I supposed, not to scare or upset them. I remember that they wrapped a hand towel around my mother's head and fastened it with an oversized safety pin along the side, where my mother's cheek must have been. I watched as they wheeled the wrapped-up bundle on its gurney down the hall, onto the freight elevator, and away.

In the room, just her hairbrush with some silvery hairs—and a wet spot on the mattress where her body had been.

Perhaps the grief I experienced in the years that followed made some sense. My mother was the only one in the family who seemed to have some appreciation of the intense and messy, complicated person that I was. Even I didn't have much hope for me—but she seemed to.

In what remained of my twenties I did the things of that time—the late 60s/early 70s—and that place—New York City. I worked, married, had a child, a divorce, a political cause or two, but all without lightness, without joy. Nothing eased the steady drone of that pain: my mother died—my mother died—she's gone—she's gone.

Eleven years passed and my search for relief was still going on. I was in the ashram of Swami Muktananda in upstate New York at summer's end, 1976. There was a woman with whom I wanted to stay in touch when we got back to town. We each had a piece of paper on which to write the other's name. On her paper Madeleine wrote "Winifred Stone."

She looked at the paper, looked at me, back to the paper again. "Ganga, wasn't your name Ingrid before Baba gave you Ganga? So who on earth is Winifred Stone?"

Time froze and I looked at the paper too. Madeleine was a tiny little woman—five feet tall at most. Her handwriting went with her body, meticulous, minute—two lines of tiny printing where I'd put one. But my mother had had a big woman's body, five feet ten or eleven, and a big woman's bold hand.

The "Winifred Stone" on Madeleine's paper was in Winifred's hand.

That is why I write to you today, dear reader. Because you may be, as I was, vulnerable to years of lost life—years stolen by grief all because of a misunderstanding so commonly held in our culture about what happens to the *person* when the body dies.

That "Winifred Stone" on a slip of paper let me know that

whatever my mother might be now, she was not nonexistent. She had not been extinguished like a candle or a cigarette butt. She had perhaps been transferred out of town. But she had not been annihilated. And that was no small difference. To my grieving heart, that was all the difference in the world.

Maui, April 27, 1993

START
the
CONVERSATION

INTRODUCTION

THE PURPOSE OF THIS BOOK
AND HOW IT CAME TO BE

W HEN I RAN INTO my old friend Ana a while ago,
I told her I was teaching a course called Start
the Conversation, a course in how to understand and prepare for death. Ana said, with obvious amuse-
ment but some exasperation too, "Oh, Ganga, you've been
trying to talk to perfectly healthy people about death for
twenty years now."

We both had a good laugh because it was true. I *have*
been trying to talk about death with all kinds of perfectly
healthy people for at least twenty years now. And as you can
probably imagine, sensible, healthy people have been avoiding me in droves the whole time.

In this book I want to have a conversation with you about
death, a different kind of conversation than you've ever had
before. It is based on a six-week course about death called
Start the Conversation that I began offering in 1989.

My best friend Michael had been diagnosed with AIDS.
Both of us had observed that while there were a number of
places to learn about the latest treatments and to talk about
healing (both physical and spiritual), there was no place to
have even the simplest, most basic conversation about death.
Yet death was the one overriding concern for Michael, as for
many of his friends.

I had become deeply interested in the nature of death because of the experience with my mother. I'd spent twenty-five years studying what is known about death in the scientific tradition of the West and the religious traditions of the East and West. I am unshakably convinced that the physical event we call death marks a transition, a passage of the spirit away from the body. Death is the moment of separation, a mere fork in the road, at which two very intimate friends part company. The spirit goes on and the body stops. What we are is spirit. We survive.

I know, really know, that there is nothing about death to be afraid of. Yet what I saw as I visited my friends in intensive care units and emergency rooms was the face of terror, again and again. Everyone was so afraid to die. It broke my heart.

Because of this unnecessary suffering, I began to have informal conversations—very cautiously at first—with people who knew they might be dying soon, my friends with AIDS in particular. These conversations relieved their fear. And their grief mellowed into sadness, which in turn yielded to a new focus on the sweetness of daily life, savored so much more fully without that awful fear.

Michael thought I ought to offer these conversations as a course, and that's how we began. When, a year after start-up, the first home of Start the Conversation relocated, I was invited to continue at Friends In Deed, a support center for people with AIDS and cancer. That's where we've been for the past six years.

Cynthia O'Neal, who founded and runs Friends, tells me that it is easy to tell who has taken the course and who has not. Those who have not go through their body's disintegration with the "normal" panic, anger and dismay. But our students experience the same process so very differently: they are confident about the outcome, so much more relaxed about all the physical changes and not the least bit reluctant to go after the pain relief that a good quality of life requires. Depression is very rare.

Reading through this book is just like taking my class. Together, we will be working on a kind of jigsaw puzzle. We'll turn up the individual pieces and I'll show you where they fit. But you'll piece the picture together for yourself. That way, you'll build your *own* conviction that there is no death. When you need that conviction, as one day you must, it will be there for you.

I like to joke with my students that I can clear a path to the bar or the buffet at any crowded party just by mentioning loudly to anyone at all that I am a death educator.

People seem to think they're going to catch some death from me. "Listen," I always say, "you caught it from your mother. In the delivery room. Your goose is already cooked."

Death Education and Preparation Services, Inc.—Even the guys who printed my business cards looked nervous. Of course, most healthy people don't want to learn any more about death than they absolutely have to. And as for preparation, buying life insurance is about as far as most people want to go—and even that only as a kind of charm against ever actually qualifying to harvest those dollars.

We just don't want to die. We don't want anybody we love to die. We don't want to think about it, talk about it or have anything to do with it. This is especially true of mothers with young children and of people newly in love. I've noticed that mothers *do* think about it, though, and worry about it constantly—"Dear God, please don't let my children die."

So we stuff death under the living room rug or into the closet, and spend our lives tiptoeing around it, or tripping over it, or trying to pretend it's not there. Where death is concerned, we assume the ostrich position: heads in the sand and bare behinds in the breeze. Dignified pose!

There's a reason for the dread, of course, and the denial. We really do believe that death is the end of the line. And if it were, no amount of fear would be excessive. And no grief could possibly be sufficient.

Listen, death is a transition. We all survive. Of this I am absolutely sure. By the time you finish this lively and enjoyable book, you'll be sure too. Knowing the truth about death will set you free. Indeed it will—free to live fearlessly, exuberantly, richly and without grief.

SEEING THROUGH THE CAMOUFLAGE

Here is a little story told me by a retired judge: "I was in the army in the last war. My job was to fly low over the countryside spotting the tanks and small aircraft that were concealed under camouflage cloth on the ground. You see," he said, "I'm color-blind, and so I can't see the camouflage. I can only see the shape of the thing as it is."

There are so many excellent and fascinating books on death, many of which have been published in the last few years. Some of these provide the raw data we'll be referring to and others provide in-depth scholarly analysis, not only of the near-death phenomenon itself, but also of the many intriguing theories that have been wrought to try to explain it.

Each contribution to the field comprises one piece of a huge jigsaw puzzle. It's the puzzle of all time: what is the real nature of death? The truth of the matter is indeed to be found in bits and pieces scattered throughout all these books. But the truth is camouflaged—effectively so—by the overabundance of information and theory that these texts contain. There are just too many pieces to sort through.

The problem, of course, is that if you have to get a handle on death rapidly—if there's been an emergency or a hard diagnosis—you'll be too shocked to read and to think. And if you run your eyes over all those titles in the death section of your bookstore, all you'll see is the camouflage.

There has been no single simple book that extracts these fragments of the truth and presents them in an orderly, logical sequence that anyone can follow and understand. Now there is.

What this book will do is walk you through the process I went through: together we will turn up only those pieces of the puzzle that are part of the picture I see, that I want to share with you.

We will leave many of the currently popular texts, especially the Tibetan Buddhist and Hindu writings, facedown on the table—not because they don't reflect the truth, but because to the Western mind, which is what most of us have, they camouflage it. For most of us, these books don't readily reveal the shape of the thing as it is.

Anyone who has been trained, as I had the good fortune to be, in Eastern thought, will see in a flash that there's nothing at all new in what I have to say. Someone once accused my teacher, Swami Muktananda, of purveying principles that were old hat. Baba chuckled and pointed out that the truth hadn't changed at all in twelve thousand years.

There is, of course, nothing new under the sun. All I am doing here is combining facts, ideas and mundane observations in a way that will make sense to a contemporary American person, a regular person like myself who reads newspapers and magazines, goes to the occasional movie, and looks for wisdom, whatever that might be, in the context of everyday life.

This book is designed both as first aid for people who have a death-related emergency and for those of you who have reason to suspect that you too will be dying one day, as will everyone you love.

The principles I present are not bolstered by large numbers of examples and references because I want these basic principles to stand out easily and clearly from the jumble of ideas on that bookshelf I spoke of earlier. In other words, I made a deliberate choice not to be exhaustive in illustrating and documenting each point.

Some books that will allow you to deepen your knowledge if you wish are suggested at the end of most chapters. There are also some very entertaining Hollywood movies that flesh out my concepts wonderfully well and are great fun besides. I'll be mentioning these, too, if renting movies is something you like to do.

The shift in perception this book will bring you cannot eliminate sadness. It does not eliminate the richness and poignancy of human life. Nothing could. We *will* surely be separated from those we love and these separations will come at any time. But you will have a different context in which to experience them and they will not wipe you out!

The immediate usefulness of this book will depend on the urgency of your situation. If you're taking care of someone who is dying, you will be able to be much more fully present. You won't have to fight off your own fear just to walk into the room. You'll know there's nothing scary going on. And you won't have to fight through grief to force a smile. You will be able to share your tears also, so your dying friend will know your sadness, which reflects your love.

If you yourself expect to be dying soon, I'm so glad you found this book now. It will comfort you. A student and friend who died recently comes to mind. John was a regular guy from Oklahoma, a sweet and quiet young man. His body broke down dramatically in his last two years. He coped with blindness, massive weight loss, indignities of all kinds. But he had no fear. He just dealt calmly with whatever the physical challenges were. He made sure he was well medicated for pain. He didn't suffer unnecessarily.

John had been taking the course for four years and I loved him a lot. I asked him why he didn't call me more often or at all, for that matter. "What would be the need?" he said. "I have the tools you gave me. That's quite enough."

You may not need these tools right now. So think of this book as life insurance. Most of us who buy life insurance are not quite ready to have our loved ones collect on it. However, when the time comes, we're awfully glad to know it's there. Even if this book is of no immediate interest, it will be at some point. Every one of us *will* need this knowledge someday.

There is *literally* no such thing as death. That is the truth of the matter. That is the shape of the thing as it is. Now, let's get going.

CHAPTER ONE

It's Not Fair

S OMEONE YOU LOVE IS DYING. Perhaps that someone is you. You just got word in the doctor's office or over the phone. There's been an awful accident, a deadly diagnosis. Oh, no!

What comes up right after the "Oh, no" is some variation of "It's not fair." And if you're like most of us, it will sound this way: "Why me? Why this? Why now?"

Now this is the hardest part of our conversation to bear. Hang in here. What I have to say is true and we all know it. The only possible answer to those three questions is "Why not?"

Find the piece of paper that guarantees you or anyone you love—partner, parent, lover, child—a long life, a healthy life. Can't find it in your wallet? Must have put it in the important papers folder in the safe. Can't find it in the safe? Can't find it anywhere? I can't find mine either.

The truth is that there *is* no such document. Look, you probably have a lease on your apartment. Or you have the title to your home. You have either lease papers or the title to your car. These documents spell out the terms under which you may live in your home or drive your car.

You know you can lie down in your bedroom at night

and your landlord will not be coming in to disturb you—most certainly not before the term of your lease expires. Even though he's the owner of the property, he has no right to throw you out. If he tried to, you could take him to court. And you would win.

However, the body, of which we're all so fond and to which we are so attached, can be reclaimed by its manufacturer at any time. When our occupancy is up, it's up. There doesn't have to be any advance notice or due process. There is no recourse, no appeal.

The actual contract, so to speak, that governs our use of these bodies reads something like this:

LEASE

Fine new body leased to Jane Jones for her temporary use.

Terms of lease: Expires at any time, at the manufacturer's discretion.

Obligations of lease: Body must be maintained by leaseholder at her own expense. Any improvements must be relinquished when the body is.

Termination of lease: Anytime, anyplace, no notice required, no appeals necessarily heard, leaseholder must vacate the premises on the spot, ready or not.

Now, if you had agreed to terms like these around your apartment, your house or your car, wouldn't you at least have made some contingency plans—say, a toothbrush and change of underwear in a little bag by the door? An extra pair of walking shoes in the trunk of the car?

We just don't want to notice the conditions that govern our use of the body even though the reminders keep coming at us. When you stood up before a judge, a rabbi, priest or minister and promised to love your spouse "till death us do part," did you think the minister was anticipating his own demise?

When you were handed the birth certificate of your first-born child, did you not notice, in the joy of the moment, the death certificate, time and place still blank, faintly inscribed on the other side?

HOW LONG HAS THIS BEEN GOING ON?

The truth of the matter is that the mortality rate of the human race has been 100 percent to date. That means all the children, all the women, all the men. We have no reasonable expectation whatsoever of getting any body out of here alive. *No* body gets out of here alive. If you think you are some *body*, this is very bad news. If you already know that you are not this body, it's no big deal.

If you are aware that this body can be recalled by the manufacturer any time at all, it somehow helps a great deal. Here's an example of what I mean.

TOBY'S STORY

On the beach one summer, I was hanging out with a group of moms while our kids splashed around in the warm, shallow bay. We got talking about mortality, and, this being my main interest, I was fascinated to hear that one of the women had given birth, six years before, to a little boy who had such a complex array of congenital problems that he was unable to stay in his impossible little body. He had died after three heartbreaking months: a fully alert, obviously intelligent little being who just wasn't dealt a playable hand and who had folded it, appropriately, early in the game. One of the moms asked Toby how she was doing now, whether she had gotten over her loss or was still grieving for her son. Here's what Toby said:

"I don't grieve at all anymore—though for the first several months I was such a mess. I just wandered around the city and wept. Then one afternoon I found myself in the Museum of Natural History—honestly, I have no idea how I even got there. But here was this big exhibit on the life cycle of the grasshopper. You couldn't miss it.

"Now I have no particular interest in grasshoppers or in any other bugs. But I stood there anyway, in what was then my usual heavy daze, waiting for the impulse to wander off to something else. In a little while, though, the details of this grasshopper exhibit began to come into focus. This is what I saw.

"Mother grasshoppers have to produce thousands and thousands of eggs just to ensure that a few individuals survive. Not every egg is viable, so she makes many, many. That's her destiny. That's the way it's always been.

"That's the way it is for us, too, that's what I finally understood. I had been immersed in the fine detail—my own tiny corner of the world—my own grief. And what excruciating grief it was. But at that moment the camera pulled back [Toby's a filmmaker], the frame got much bigger and the new picture, the big picture, took my breath away.

"This has been going on for eons. That's what took my grief away, too—the sense of where my baby and my husband and I fit in. And that there was a place in the natural order of things for us and for our son."

In class, I sometimes share Toby's story, and I point out that in many parts of the world, couples have to bring seven or eight babies into the world just to see two or three of them into adolescence. So it is and so it will be, for so it has been, time out of mind. That's the contract. Those are the terms.

But how we can suffer when we don't read the contract thoroughly and require ourselves to think its implications through.

NO BODY GETS OUT OF HERE ALIVE

I was asked to visit a local family in which the eighty-two-year-old mother was dying of a cancer she'd been struggling with for about five years. She and her husband had been very happily married for over fifty years—the sort of marriage we somehow don't expect to see fifty years from now, full of steady companionship and a deep familiarity that miraculously hadn't bred contempt.

There were three grown children, two daughters and a son; one of the daughters was visiting on the day I dropped in. Here's how the visit went:

DAUGHTER: This is so terrible—I don't know what we're going to do.

HUSBAND/FATHER: What did she do to deserve such suffering?

DAUGHTER: We can't understand why this has to happen.

HUSBAND/FATHER: We've been so happy all these years—
this just isn't fair!

Now, I have oversimplified their remarks, but not by much. You get the picture. Perhaps it sounds familiar, too. It's why us, why this, why now, isn't it? Well, why not? That's the real puzzle.

These folks are highly educated adults, sophisticated professionals with successful careers—people who are confident that they know what life is all about. Why me? Why this? Why now? I'm stumped. Beats me. Why not??

And this is not to make light of their suffering. It's real as real can be. But it's not the only possible response to their situation. And while we often hear "why me, why this, why now?" when someone's in the next room dying, these thoughts just don't make a whole lot of sense. This you must see.

HECTOR SPOTS THE TRUTH

I was visiting with one of God's Love We Deliver's earliest clients, a handsome, very bright Puerto Rican man named Hector. It must have been early in the spring of 1987. I was enormously pregnant with my daughter at the time, who was born in April of that year.

Hector was a charming man, full of entertaining stories and such a pleasure to be with. So I spent quite a bit of time in his company. When I describe him as handsome, though, it's based on photos he showed me that were taken before Kaposi's sarcoma (an AIDS-related skin cancer) claimed the surface of his body. Hector had become a "purple person"— that was his phrase—and was as pregnant with his death as I was with my new baby. There was no ducking the outcome of our physical conditions for either of us.

"But you know, Ganga," Hector said cheerfully out of the blue one evening, "you could die before I do!" His peppy little observation annoyed the hell out of me, and it triggered some thoughts that ran this way: 1. Not much chance of that. 2. Poor guy, he's going to be dying pretty soon. 3. That was a mean thing to say; he must be scared. 4. Odds are on my side, though.

And then, in an almost comical, lightbulb-going-on-over-the-head moment, I got it. "You know something, Hector, you're absolutely right!" And we both had a good laugh over it because he had heard my silent protests, had been in on my attempt to push his observation away with pity, with denial of my own hugely vulnerable physical state, and with a fall-back position having to do with the odds of dying sometime soon in each of our cases.

What Hector pointed out had to do with possibility, not probability. He was way ahead of me in his understanding of the terms of the lease. He saw that the possibility of being forced to move out was 100 percent, no matter what the state of one's health. It wasn't a question of what, but of when. As for when, today was as possible a day as any other. And that was equally true for both of us.

In case you are still kidding yourself that the *odds* against your death occurring today will somehow protect you, notice that the odds against winning a fat lottery jackpot are pretty long also. People do win that money, though. And notice that if you were guaranteed to win it at some point, you'd ignore the odds and buy a ticket every day, wouldn't you? Hey, you never know, right? By the way, do you buy lottery tickets? Just asking.

In New York the lottery slogan is "You gotta be in it to win it." But you can relax, you're already in it. And you will win it, too. It may be a long shot, but it *is* a sure shot, right?

If you still don't get it, here's a breathtaking story that does drive home the point, though gruesomely.

A family of four was driving along the busy stretch of highway near the George Washington Bridge in northern New Jersey. They were in a European-made station wagon advertised as the best choice from a safety standpoint, since the car is designed to protect its occupants in the event of collision. No protection from falling bowling balls, however. Here's what happened:

Some teenage boys had been foraging in a vacant lot and came upon a bowling ball. There are only so many ways to play with a bowling ball outside a bowling alley. You can't exactly kick it around or play catch with it. So maybe you drop it from an overpass onto a busy highway just to see if it will bounce. That's what they did.

And it bounced just fine—bounced off the fender of a northbound truck, bounced into the southbound lane, bounced through the windshield of that super-safe family car and struck the eight-month-old baby girl right on the head. Strike. Not a spare.

Her parents had done every single thing they could to keep her safe: she was strapped in her car seat, she was right where she belonged. And I guess the odds against death by bowling ball are excellent, especially for babies. But it happened just that way anyway, despite the odds. There was low probability of these events, to be sure. But the *possibility* that this baby would die was 100 percent. Anytime. Anyplace. Any way. Are you still with me?

WHAT ARE THE POSSIBILITIES?

Once these reminders are in place, here's what I always hear next: "But I'll miss them so much—all my friends—everybody." One young man, full of grief, said: "I lost most of my family last year."

"Well, stick around," I said. "You get to lose the rest of them or they get to lose you. What else is possible? And by the way, which would you prefer? Not that you get a vote."

LOSING THE WHOLE FAMILY

I was flipping through *People* magazine recently—something I look forward to each week, as I don't watch television and need *People* to keep up with what's going on, plus it's fun. And there was a story of several pages with many photos about the Weaver family of Upper St. Clair, Pennsylvania.

They all went down on that USAir flight to Pittsburgh that dropped out of the clear blue sky for no apparent reason last fall. Now this is hard to bear—really it is. Three sweet kids, sixteen, eleven and seven, and their parents, kind people, caring people—good to everyone in their little town—fortunate people, blessed. Gone—all together—on a clear October night. Don't you hate that? I could hardly look at the photos—such earnest, upbeat faces. Sweet people. Such a heartbreak.

But there is another side—nobody had to miss anybody. Each member of the family was spared grieving the loss of the other five—which is no small deal. There would have been ten experiences of grief had the Weavers died over many decades, one by one. In going down together, at least they escaped that suffering.

Do you get the picture? Once again, we're discussing possibilities, not probabilities. The risk of a plane going down with the whole family on board is something most of us never even contemplate. But you know, the British royal family thinks about it, since they must have at least one surviving heir to continue the family business.

So they pay attention to the fact that if it's a *possibility* for the plane to go down, planning has to reflect that possibility, no matter how slender the odds. That's why even if everybody is off to Australia for a week, they don't all climb on the same plane. They hedge their bets. There's so much at stake. So somebody takes a separate plane or stays home.

We seldom function as if the possible-though-improbable were nonetheless possible. We naturally prefer not to notice that the fine print on the contract does read: anytime, anyplace. Everybody at once or one by one.

Of course, we think that for us it really reads in our own bed, in our sleep, in our eighty-eighth year. That is our notion of the natural order of things, isn't it, despite the information coming to us via TV or the daily papers that this is not the case.

There is no question that the death of people we love hurts terribly. We'll look into the reasons for that grief in the next chapter and see if we can get a handle on it by figuring out what makes us feel so disoriented, so undone.

Usually, though, the most easily identified feature of our grief has to do with what we experience as *missing the person*.

And that's the good news, because together we can work to explore the distinction between missing people as we naturally do when they move out of town or leave our lives in some other way, and missing people painfully, desperately, as we do when someone has died. Let's call the former emotion sadness and the latter grief.

It's grief that's the real problem, isn't it? Sadness is just one of the ways we usually feel when there's change of almost any kind in our lives. But grief is a wipeout.

In the next chapter we're going to lay the groundwork for handling grief in a way that's relatively new in our culture. But it works. If you are going through a period of grief right now and are sick and tired of it, read on.

*   *   *

First, please take a minute to jot down your responses to these quick questions.

> *Today's date:*
>
> *Have you really grasped the fact that every relationship you hold dear will be interrupted—at least temporarily—by the event called death?*
>
> *If not, are you willing to try to hold that concept, at least for the duration of this conversation?*

This will help you to remember.

No Body Gets Out of Here Alive.

CHAPTER TWO

THE ANNIHILATION PREMISE: FEAR AND GRIEF

ONE EVENING IN THE early months of the Conversation, along came James. He was a handsome, high-energy actor in his early 40s, forceful, confident and very articulate. He sat down and started right in.

"Listen," he said, "I've read Hegel and I've read Kant. I've read Schopenhauer and I've read Sartre. I've read all the major Western philosophers and the minor ones too. And I can tell you, there's no possibility that anything continues after the body dies—the arguments are clear—the great thinkers all agree—you're full of shit."

Variations on this theme poured forth from James for at least twenty minutes. He was eloquent, he was convincing, he was brilliant, he was proud. He was making short work of me.

Meanwhile, I sat there thinking, *Dear God, what on earth am I going to say to this one?* There was no way I could tackle him on his own terms. And he had no room in his mind for mine. What to do?

Then it happened. James took a long breath, gripped the arms of his chair, leaned forward and paused, then into the silence his pause had created—and with fingers dug deep into the cushioned arms of his chair—blurted out, "I'm so fucking scared to die."

There was no sound in the room—my eyes filled up— my heart was breaking for James. No one spoke. I took a deep breath.

"Well, James," I said, "if you think you're scared now— you ain't seen nothin' yet. Your body is still going strong. But just wait 'til it starts breaking down. You think your body is what you are. That's why you're so fucking scared to die. If you can't see it any other way, you're going to suffer like crazy when that thing you think you are hits the rocks.

"It's your call, James. But let's not waste each other's time. If all you want to do is come here and argue, you might as well not come around!"

Now that was the toughest I'd ever been. But James did come back around. And off and on for the next two years, he read and thought, he fussed and argued, and he came to class. He made his own study of mortality and he allowed his mind to change. And though he certainly did not go gently (this was one very melodramatic guy), he did not go with fear.

Fear is the big one for most of us. And right beside it is grief. Most people in the AIDS community have buried the friends they thought they'd spend old age with—and then buried the thought of old age. Made wills instead. The grief is horribly heavy in the air. And it shows up in so many disguises—cynicism, anger, fatigue, depression, boredom, denial, despair.

Fear and grief are the thieves of joy—and of any hope of joy. Yet they rest on a single simple but false assumption— that the human being is only a body, a mere thing—and that the entire human being is destroyed with the body at death. On this tragically mistaken belief rests all the suffering—all the grief and all the fear—that make it so difficult to live out a life, of whatever duration, in freedom and in joy.

THINK ABOUT THIS

Back in the middle of the fifteenth century, every educated person KNEW that the world was flat. All the maps of that time reflected this view. It was taught in the universities, libraries were filled with volumes based on this premise and travel plans were made (or not made) accordingly.

Imagine the bookstores of the day . . . shelf after shelf of titles exploring the physical and emotional hazards of dropping off the edge. Imagine the therapists and counselors solemnly advising years of pricey treatment for fear (of falling off the edge oneself) and grief (over the imminent sailing-over-the-edge of a loved one).

Imagine that most people would elect to stay pretty close to home rather than risk falling off the edge. Imagine that a young woman would think long and hard before marrying someone whose career put him at risk of sailing over the edge.

It wasn't that the people who held these beliefs were unintelligent. All the best minds of the time believed the world was flat. And there was nothing illogical or inappropriate about the strategies they developed for coping with what was absolutely their reality. You can see where I'm heading. What makes it all seem ridiculous to you is that the underlying premise was so wrong, so utterly wrong.

THE ANNIHILATION PREMISE

Our underlying premise about death here in the West is just that mistaken. If you've never given any particular thought to death, you may not even have noticed how fully you buy into this annihilation idea.

But notice how frightened you would be if your doctor gave you just six weeks. And notice how undone by grief

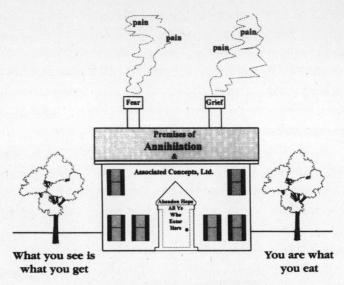

What you see is   **You are what**
what you get   **you eat**

I Am Limited to This Body

you would have been had one of your dearest friends been in that plane over Lockerbie.

This is a physical way to represent the connection between the Annihilation Premise and fear and grief. I think it makes it especially easy to understand what we have to do to get rid of the whole structure.

In this visual metaphor, we see that the two chimneys are up on the roof and the smoke that rises through them (that gets in our eyes, that makes us cry), let's just call that pain. It gets to us through those two conduits, fear and grief.

Let's knock those chimneys down, then. But we can't get at them; they're way up on the roof. Besides, even if we could knock them off the roof, the two chimneys are hooked up to a system of fireplaces that runs throughout the house. Fear and grief are an integral part, a necessary feature of the Premises of Annihilation and Associated Concepts. They have to be there. And even—just to carry the image a little further—even if we were to brick up (that is, suppress, deny or try to ignore) those fireplaces throughout the house, they'd still be there.

No, we'll have to demolish the whole house. And that's a very big expensive job (not unlike psychoanalysis). It's not guaranteed to do the trick either, as those chimneys originate in the basement anyway.

What *is* clear is that we could do the whole job by digging up the foundation on which this troublesome structure rests. Just look at the foundation. It's labeled I AM LIMITED TO THIS BODY. If we can dig out (excavate) this common belief, we are home free, because it is on this particular mistaken idea that the Annihilation Premise rests and it's the Annihilation Premise that is responsible for all the fear and all the grief—and all the suffering they cause us.

That the body begins to disintegrate when its inhabitant lets it go is obvious and inevitable. Our ingrained and usually unchallenged assumption that a human being is limited to the body is reinforced by the immediate surge of grief that swamps our little boat when someone we love has died. This is all about missing the person, that is, not having access to their physical presence, the voice, the hug, the dear, dear face, not ever seeing them again.

This experience is so stunningly painful that there's no way, as far as I know, to pull back from it enough to analyze and dismantle it. We don't think clearly when we're in so much pain; how can we? That's why it's so important to get a handle on this matter of mortality *before* we have to deal with it, not afterward.

Fear and grief seem like "natural" responses to the prospect of death. And indeed, if a precious unique human being *were* annihilated, blown away as dust, by death, what grief could ever be sufficient? What fear?

BUT THAT IS NOT WHAT HAPPENS. WE SURVIVE. AND
WE CAN PROVE IT.

We have already established that NO BODY GETS OUT
OF HERE ALIVE. So to prove that you will survive your death
I'd have to be able to show that you are not limited to or identical with your body. And to do that, I'll need your cooperation. Give it to me in the form of the following sentence:

> *I am holding open the possibility that I am not lim-*
> *ited to my body and that I might still be around, in*
> *some form or fashion, when my body dies.*

If you will just make room for that possibility, I in turn
will promise to speak logically to you. I won't ask you to
take anything on faith. All you have to do is keep your mind
working—in the open position, that is—and follow along.
So here's what we have so far:

1. *No body gets out of here alive.*

2. *I am holding open the possibility that I am not limited*
   to my body and that I might still be around, in some
   form or fashion, when my body dies.

Just to see where you are with this possibility today (I
will ask you again at the end of the book), please note your
response to the question below:

> *Date:*

> *Do you think you will die with your body?*

Now on to the next chapter where we will consider the
question "What is proof?"

CHAPTER THREE

WHAT IS PROOF?

Y OU HAVE AGREED TO hold open the possibility that you are not limited to your body—and I've said I won't ask you to take anything on faith.

That means the burden of proof rests with me, as it should. Let's begin by considering the question: what is proof? There are at least two types of proof, and within each, two ways of proving something, direct and indirect. Let's look at them one at a time.

SCIENTIFIC PROOF

Usually, when we want to prove something, our minds automatically run along a scientific track. We believe a thing can be proven to exist if, for example, we and others can see it, touch it, weigh it, hear it, smell it or taste it. If a scientist produces a result in the laboratory, her colleagues expect to be able to replicate it. If they can, then the result has been proven and can be accepted. This is *direct* proof.

Clearly, direct scientific proof works well when what we're considering is something concrete that we can get access to. But suppose what we're trying to demonstrate can't be examined *directly* in any physical way. Is there another way within the domain of science to prove that something is true? Can we show that something exists if it cannot be weighed or measured?

INDIRECT PROOF

We can infer the existence of something by measuring its effects. Some branches of science—astronomy, for example— have at times the option to *infer* the reality of a phenomenon. The black hole, for example, can be identified *indirectly* by observing its gravitational effects on nearby structures in deep space. But in order to have confidence in their conclusion that such a thing as a black hole exists, the astronomers will have to *rule out* all other possible explanations for the effects they observe through their amazing radio telescopes.

Note that the only way to test a hypothesis would be to see if you can use it consistently to *predict* how something will behave. Note these two ideas: we'll be coming back to this in the next chapter when we explore the significance of the aftereffects of the near-death experience. Now let's consider the nonscientific method of proving things. Here we're all on very familiar ground.

LEGAL PROOF

Our legal system is based on a very different way of proving things than the scientific way. It depends for *direct* proof on eyewitness accounts—it depends on the firsthand testimony of reliable witnesses. We all know the way this works.

A panel of twelve individuals, a jury, is appointed. This is a diverse group, usually having just one important thing in common: a willingness to hold no prior opinion about the matter at hand. They will listen impartially and carefully to what each witness has to say. And the witnesses in turn are sworn to tell the truth.

If all the witnesses tell substantially the same story and if no one has come forward with a good reason not to believe them (this is called "reasonable doubt"), then the legal system, which is the structural basis of our society, rules that the matter has been proven.

Now notice especially that even though no one *on the jury* was present when the disputed event took place, we are able legally to prove that it happened by hearing direct eyewitness accounts—the testimony of people who *were* there and are not lying.

Indirect Proof

Now suppose no one actually saw the event. Everything gets much more complicated in such a case because our system is designed to protect an innocent person from false judgment based merely on circumstances that make it *look* as if he or she did the deed. The burden of proof lies with the accusers, as we all know. And they must prove, again beyond all *reasonable* doubt, that our presumably innocent person was the only person on the planet who could have done the deed *and* that he or she was not elsewhere at the time, i.e., there is no alibi.

Here's where expert testimony comes in: the fingerprint specialist who tells us those are indeed the accused person's unique prints, the DNA expert who identifies the hair or the blood beyond all reasonable doubt. Notice that even when there are *no* eyewitnesses to tell us what they saw, we can prove someone guilty if *objectively verifiable* facts are presented.

And just to underscore how seriously we take this

process, note that people can lose their freedom, if not their lives, if their guilt has been proven in this way.

What we propose to prove is that the human being is not limited to the merely physical. To do so, we will turn to the perfectly sound methods of legal proof.

As we go along in this discussion, I will ask you to consider what is presented from your seat in the jury box. Remember that the people whose stories you will hear have promised to tell the truth. And remember that you have no prior opinion about the matter we are setting out to prove, which is that something—we may not know what it is, but something very real—survives the process of transition we call death.

So now we have:

1. *No body gets out of here alive.*

2. *I am holding open the possibility that I am not limited to my body and that I might still be around, in some form or fashion, when my body dies.*

3. *I will listen to the firsthand accounts of reliable witnesses and then see what I think.*

CHAPTER FOUR

MAKING SENSE OF THE NEAR-DEATH EXPERIENCE

WE TALKED ABOUT THE near-death experience one evening in class. I showed a video about the NDE, offering the firsthand accounts of four adults and six children. The kids were especially touching, extending their off-handed, casual reassurances to the pediatrician interviewing them. "You'll see, Dr. Morse, it's FUN to be there." One little girl said: "I was, like, free, you know?" And the mother of another child reported that her daughter has a mission now (her daughter was eight or so). All this otherwise regular little girl wants to do now is talk to little children who are very sick so that they won't have to be so afraid to die.

The adults were a giggly group. One woman said: "I was much more alive dead!" And another observed: "This world's a school—and I'll be glad when I graduate."

Raymond Moody, the originator of near-death studies, has summarized the effect of this experience on all the thousands of people he has interviewed. "Of course," he said, *"it absolutely eliminates their fear of death."*

Of course. The reason it absolutely eliminates their fear of death is that it irrevocably destroys the Annihilation Premise.

Remember that it is the Annihilation Premise that gives rise to both fear and grief. It is just *impossible* to scare someone about death when they have seen that, though the body was out of business, they were still themselves: reasoning, feeling, seeing and hearing, amazed, but alive.

What would it take to ABSOLUTELY ELIMINATE your fear of death? How many firsthand accounts would you need to hear before what you *think* about death began to shift, and how many more would you need to hear before what you *know* about death was forever changed? How many?

Thirteen million of our friends and neighbors, our fellow Americans, have had this experience by now (read George Gallup, Jr.'s *Adventures in Immortality*). Resuscitation techniques have become sophisticated and commonplace. Even small town hospitals have what it takes to shock a dead body back into life.

As a group, near-death experiencers have nothing in common except having been clinically dead. This is about as random a sample of the population as can be. Every religious, racial, social and educational level is well represented. But here, in the words of one woman, a nurse by profession, is what all near-death experiencers know:

> *First, I know that death is not painful. I will never be afraid to die. And I know that when you die you are not snuffed out. I know that I'm more than my body. There's a soul that's me. And I know that I, my soul, will always be there. I know for certain that there is life after death.*
>
> Life, *March 1993*

Did you notice her choice of verb? I *know*, not I think, not I believe, but I *know*. This is not an opinion, this is an absolute conviction, based on personal experience, that she is more than her body, a conviction that what she calls her soul—who she really is—will always be there.

And because the Annihilation Premise has been demolished irrevocably for her, this woman has the marvelous certainty that she will never be afraid to die. What an amazing life she is now free to lead.

Let's hear from a few of the thirteen million Americans who have had this life-transforming experience we call the NDE. Remember that you are seated in the jury box and remember too that the people you are going to listen to have no reason to lie. Here we go.

FRANK AND LILY'S TALE

Frank is a brilliant Oxford-trained economist who is a professor at an Ivy League school, and also works with the World Bank and some Far Eastern governments as an expert in economic development. I met him at a conference in Hilton Head, South Carolina, where I was presenting a much-condensed version of my six-week course. (They gave me ten whole minutes.)

Frank's wife Lily was in the front row at my presentation. She drew my attention by her stillness and her grave expression. We spoke at some length afterward. That's when I learned that Lily had been sitting right beside her husband when he died, so to speak. Though this had happened three years before, there were, not surprisingly, remnants of the shock in her restrained manner and her wide-eyed, vulnerable-looking face. She moved and spoke as if something precious inside her might break—or had already broken and mustn't ever break again. Here's the story from Frank's point of view. We'll revisit Lily later, when we have another look at grief.

"I was playing squash with a regular partner of mine. It was about ninety or ninety-five degrees, and we played for over two hours in that heat, foolishly. After playing, I went and took a shower and just began to feel dreadful. I denied, for quite some time—like an hour or so—what was going on, until it became virtually impossible to deny that something was seriously wrong.

"At first, I tried to say it was just the heat or dehydration. But there I was, lying naked in this locker room on this bench, not doing a very good job of telling everybody I was really just fine.

"And finally, someone actually overruled me, because they kept asking me, 'Are you sure you don't want to go to the hospital and get some help?' And I said, 'I don't need any help.' Someone overruled me. Lily showed up and an ambulance showed up. They took me to the hospital and then they told me, 'You're having a heart attack.' And then they gave me the clot-busting drug.

"Things seemed to be getting better and they moved me into an intensive care unit. Lily and I were sitting quietly together talking and then suddenly, my heart simply stopped beating. That was it. Just nothing.

"The alarms went off because they had me wired up. And apparently, people came running over. They went about their business, as it were. And I was unaware of them.

"I had a number of sensations. So many terms are used to describe dying—'crossing over, passing away.' What I experienced was a joining or, really more aptly, a rejoining.

"It didn't *matter* to me that I was losing my body. It didn't *matter* to me that I was losing my ego, that 'I,' as it were. There was a wonderful sense of almost divine composure. There was a sense of beckoning, of being drawn into some place that was immensely appealing. There was a sense of shedding burdens, *no matter* how happily or gladly taken on, there was a sense of relief at the shedding of those burdens.

"There was a sense of returning to the most blissful, childlike position imaginable, of being in a place of total security, enveloped by my love, cut off from any concerns or fears.

"There was no fear, at which I was a little surprised because I was aware of what was going on, but THERE WAS NO FEAR. It was just, of course, this is just as natural as can be, and it feels like it must have felt when I emerged into this world.

"One of the blessings of this experience, for me, is that the lack of fear has remained. I fear not, and that lack of fear—it has not only freed me from the fear of death, but it's opened me up to life in a way that's left me feeling very grateful."

No Matter

Frank's life feels very different to him now, since he is without the fear that keeps most of us marching so carefully between the lines, avoiding risk of any kind. What was Frank's fear based on? It was based on the Annihilation Premise. Notice how he kept saying things didn't *matter*—basic things that matter to most of us: losing the body and its relatives, its friends, losing the career, losing all those wonderfully compelling burdens so happily taken on. Relief at letting those burdens go. Relief, not sorrow, not even ambivalence. Relief.

It seems that once we know we are *not* matter, nothing that *is* matter *can* matter. Frank was home free, for one moment. That's what his gratitude is about. And he will never be afraid again.

Now here is an account from someone whose near-death experience took place when he was so young that the fear of death never arose in him at all.

MATTHEW'S STORY

Matt came to Start the Conversation at my request to share his near-death experience with the students. He is an elementary schoolteacher by profession, though he had hoped, as one of eight children in an Irish-Catholic family, that he would build himself a life away from the din of kids.

Matt's near-death adventure happened in the rough-and-tumble neighborhood of his early childhood. A number of his buddies were playing the sort of game that makes parents cringe: they were throwing rocks at each other in a mock warfare of the sort boys seem to like to do. One sizable chunk of boulder clocked five-year-old Matt on the skull, making a substantial dent on the right side of it. In fact, that side of his skull was crushed like a grape, says Matt.

He was instantaneously outside his body, seeing the bloody mess on the ground beside his head, seeing the terrified face of the boy who had thrown the rock, seeing his parents scurrying about, scooping his body up and into the ambulance.

Then Matt found himself, without his body, of course, following along after the ambulance, though he had, as he said afterward, no particular investment in the bloody body it carried. He reported watching as the doctors struggled to coax him back into a situation in which he had very little interest.

Afterward, Matt offered intricate details of the complex

gyrations his doctors had gone through to repair his skull and restart his body. His parents were baffled, as of course the doctors were too, that Matt had such precise knowledge of what had been done, or that he had any knowledge at all, since as far as they knew, he was gone. He was certainly not conscious, not in the usual sense.

After Matt told his story, which included a very sweet encounter with a being he recognized as Jesus, Matt took questions from the group. One student, a woman with quite extensive cancer who was working to get a handle on her fear, asked Matt whether he himself had any fear of death.

There was a pause before he answered, and then a slightly puzzled-sounding Matt said: "Why, no, I don't have any fear of death. I've never been happier or more myself than when I was dead."

When I asked him afterward what the hesitation had been and why he had seemed confused by the question, he said: "You know, I think that because my NDE happened when I was so small, I just never learned to be scared of death. That's why the question threw me for a minute—I couldn't really get what she was asking about. It is so utterly outside my experience. *I can't even imagine what being afraid to die might be like.*"

This utter absence of fear of death is the hallmark of the near-death experiencer. It is such a profound distinction, though an invisible one, that it truly marks the near-death survivor as radically different from the rest of us. Nothing could be stranger, and until now, rarer, in the so-called normal world than a person who is genuinely unafraid of death.

So we have an *effect,* fearlessness, of which the near-death experience is the only uniform *cause.* And if we predict that someone who has had a near-death experience will be unafraid of death *forever,* not just for a few months, we'll be right—in every case. Something real is going on. These people know without a doubt that they survived. They know we all will.

Graduates of the near-death experience know that they were alive and well even though their bodies were not. They never worry about death again. I could relate many, many similar stories. If you'd like more examples, there's a list of books to read at the end of this chapter. The most important thing to note here is that near-death experiencers are forever unafraid of death.

But does this give *you* enough confidence to face your own death without fear? It doesn't? Let's see why not.

THE CORROBORATING WITNESS

The difficulty most of us have in believing that the near-death experience proves survival is that these experiences seem to take place, just as dreams do, inside somebody else's head. If only there were some solid bridge between the landscape of the NDE (the tunnel, the being of light, and the like) and our own familiar solid "real" world. Let's see if we can build one. Here we turn to the legal method of proof to make our point.

Recently a reporter from *People* magazine called to verify a few facts for an article she was working on. She was after the name of someone who could verify my account of events that had taken place twenty-two years before. And it had to be a person who had actually been there.

Without that corroborating eyewitness, the information couldn't be used in her article because there wouldn't be a way to prove that I was telling the truth. Without corroboration, even from just one other person, my story could not successfully be defended in court if it were challenged.

People magazine wasn't even slightly interested in losing a libel suit. Of course.

Now isn't that interesting? All the reporter needed to protect herself and her employer was one eyewitness, one person to say, "Yes, I was there and saw that, too." Well. . . . So all our legal system needs to make a tight case is the word of one credible eyewitness.

Can we verify the near-death experience in the same way? Absolutely! But to do that, we'll need the testimony of someone reliable who has checked out the details of the story of a person fresh back from death and was able to say, "Yes, I saw that, too."

But saw what, too? The tunnel, the being of light, the long-dead relatives and friends? Not likely. Not even possible. But what if our near-death experiencer saw and heard details of the here and now—heard conversations, for example, taking place in another part of the hospital or saw objects that were not even in the room where their unconscious body lay?

What if young children could describe complex procedures that had been performed on their comatose bodies? What if someone came back from the NDE with details like that AND what if those details could be verified by someone on the scene? Would we have proof that we are not limited to the body then? Listen to these accounts and see what you think.

THE SNEAKER ON THE LEDGE

There's Maria, a middle-aged woman whose heart quit working while she was in a Seattle hospital. To her amazement, she found herself—not her body, to be sure, but her self—floating around the hospital while a team of doctors struggled successfully to restart her heart.

Afterward, the hospital sent over Kim Clark, a social worker, to help Maria adjust to life with a seriously damaged heart. But Maria wasn't interested in that conversation. She needed to prove to herself and to anyone else she could that she wasn't crazy—that she had indeed separated from her body.

Maria told the social worker that she had seen a shoe, a sneaker, in fact, on the ledge outside a window three floors above the room her body had been confined to when her heart clicked off. To get the essential reality check, Maria asked that Kim find that window and see if the sneaker were there—not just any sneaker either, but an old one, with a worn little toe and one lace tucked under the heel.

Kim humored her and went up three floors, as Maria requested, and over two rooms to the spot Maria had described. She opened the appropriate window and there indeed lay the sneaker on the ledge, all by itself (who can imagine *how* it got there), worn little toe and all.

What do you make of that? Maria's observation was corroborated by her very skeptical social worker. Maria's body had been flat on its back in the coronary care unit, with its heart (eyes, too, of course) out of commission when Maria-not-limited-to-her-body saw the sneaker on the hospital ledge.

And by the way, there were no other tall buildings anywhere near Harborview Hospital. To see that sneaker on the ledge would have required a telescope set up in the nearest high-rise several miles away. So.

The implications of this corroboration are very important to our case. Let's label this and all such phenomena a Sneaker on the Ledge. Here's what that is.

A Sneaker on the Ledge is an observation in the physical realm, that is, the "real world" that:

a) *could not possibly have been* physically *seen or heard by the person who tells us about it and*

b) *has been verified by a reliable second person.*

For reliable verification, what could be more convenient than the doctor who worked on the resuscitation? Here's an account by Melvin Morse, whose eleven-year-old patient described the goings-on during his twenty-minute cardiac arrest:

> *He accurately described his own resuscitation, as though he really watched it from outside his body. An eleven-year-old cannot describe an emergency room resuscitation with any great accuracy, no matter how much television he watches.*
>
> *He was able to describe the positions and colors of the instruments around the room, the gender of the attending physicians and even what they said during this frantic procedure.*

What are we to make of these accounts? I have presented just two, both for simplicity's sake and because I think that even these two examples of Sneaker on the Ledge phenomena serve to more than make the point.

And the point is this: Something or, more properly, someone left the body behind and saw things without using the body's eyes, heard conversations without using the body's ears, and thought and remembered things without using the body's brain.

REASONABLE DOUBT

Reasonable doubt, my lawyer friends tell me, is doubt for which you can state a good reason. Evidently one's opinion that something is "just not possible" does not constitute reasonable doubt. Get this.

I recently heard Sherwin Nuland, the surgeon who wrote *How We Die,* interviewed on CNN. The interviewer asked whether Dr. Nuland thought there were any possibility whatsoever that a human being might have some component part that was NOT the body and that might survive death.

"Absolutely not," Dr. Nuland said. "That's just not possible!" Then he added, "I have to think this way. It's the only way I can keep my ducks in a line and my stars hanging in the firmament."

At that point, he outlined a little box in the air with both hands. It defined a block of air about one foot square within which Dr. Nuland proposed to keep his ducks in a line. As far as I can tell, this is NOT called reasonable doubt, that is, doubt for which there is a sound reason.

SEEING THROUGH THE CAMOUFLAGE

Though there are certainly some scientists who insist that the near-death experience must be the result of biochemical or neurophysiological disturbances in the brain or a lack of oxygen to the brain, you can see that there is no way such ideas can explain a Sneaker on the Ledge.

What chemical shift in the brain, indeed, what circumstances of any kind, can provide someone with information about what's going on in another part of town? When the body is incapable of functioning, even temporarily, but the person nonetheless has experiences that are checked out by a reliable witness, we must conclude that there is something, or someone, that is not confined to or limited by the body. Though it (the survivor, soul, essence, spirit or whatever name you prefer) lives in the body, it can go on without the body. And it does.

That there is no other explanation for these Sneaker on the Ledge phenomena is critical, of course. Often what scientists, physicians and others offer to refute the possibility that something exists independently of the body is the idea that the person wasn't really—that is, irreversibly—dead yet.

MORE CAMOUFLAGE

Doesn't that sound logical, doesn't that sound important? But take a closer look. All we need to demonstrate, in order to get the Annihilation Premise out of our heads for good, is that human beings are not limited to the body. By "limited to the body," we mean:

- *able to function* only *within the limits of the physical senses.*

- *able to see* only *with the physical eyes and* only *that which is within range of the physical eyes.*

- *able to hear* only *with the physical ears and* only *that which is within range of the physical ears.*

Now, the reason our near-death experiencers were being worked over by a bunch of medical folks is that they were presumed dead—as in no heartbeat, no breathing, no blood pressure, no newspapers, no movies, no TV—nothing going on in the physical apparatus at all. That was the problem in the first place, remember?

So the ability to report conversations in another part of the hospital or to see and remember phenomena that were nowhere near the nearly dead body just *cannot be explained* using pseudoscientific jargon. It cannot be discounted, dismissed or disallowed by a collection of well but narrowly trained minds whose main business it is to "keep their ducks in a line," especially if they have to violate their own rules of logic and reason to do so.

THE SHAPE OF THE THING AS IT IS

Just to nail it for you, one last point. Elisabeth Kübler-Ross, the pioneering Swiss-born physician who opened the entire field of death and dying to serious study twenty-five years ago and who has personally had countless experiences that have convinced her that human survival is a fact, makes the following statement in one of her recently published books. And this is the ultimate Sneaker on the Ledge example, I think.

Dr. Kübler-Ross reports that she has questioned several totally blind near-death experiencers—people without even minimal light perception—and found that they could describe minute details of their successful resuscitations, details like the stripes on a tie, the color of a shirt or a jacket, who came into the room and when.

These details could never have been observed under so-called normal circumstances, as the blind observer had no capacity to see anything—not even light and shadow, much less the patterns on a tie.

CAN WE GET THIS?

Just because arriving at the conclusion that a human person is not subject to death as we once believed—just because that conclusion totally changes the way we see the world, the way we live our lives, the way we anticipate our deaths, just because it's hard to shift a belief that's been sitting in our brains (and in Western culture) forever doesn't mean we can't do it. We certainly can. And we must.

Here's a definition of humility that I heard a while ago:

> *Humility isn't putting yourself down; that's just putting yourself down. Humility is knowing that you could learn something in the very next moment that would totally change the way you see the world.*

I like that—"totally change the way you see the world." What could be more exciting? Especially if what this changed view provides is a way to push the two biggest obstacles to having a good life—that is, fear and grief—forever out of our way.

It's a radical shift we're looking at here—that is, a shift at the very roots of our belief system. But once we make this shift, everything comes together in a brand-new way, a much more enjoyable way, you'll see.

IT'S ROUND AFTER ALL

Back to that flat-world to round-world shift we spoke of earlier. That was certainly as enormous, in terms of the way people understood their universe and lived their lives, as the shift we're after here.

But you know, once Columbus brought his three little boats safely home, nobody suggested that he go out again and again just to make sure his results were real. No. Columbus's safe return, with a few pieces of physical proof that he had been someplace brand-new—a few Sneakers on the Ledge, if you will—was sufficient.

There was no edge to sail over after all. He proved it. And knowing there was money to be made, the king and queen of Spain invested in a fleet of ships for Columbus, not just three modest little tubs, so he could travel farther and bring back more.

A LITTLE HUMILITY

My point is this: There was no hesitation to believe what his successful return had proven or, seen another way, there was sufficient humility—sufficient awareness that we just *can't* know the whole story about *everything*—to allow a total rethinking and reconceptualizing of the nature of the physical world.

Certainly the way maps were drawn was changed for good. In Germany right around this time, a man named Martin Behaim produced the first map of the newly round world—the first globe. Columbus's victory certainly changed the way commerce was conducted, literally opening a "new world" to be explored.

Let's say it also altered the way sailors assessed their risks and the risks assumed by people who loved them. This new knowledge must have eliminated irrational fear and its attendant grief. Knowledge is supposed to do that. If we make room for it, it does.

BUILDING YOUR OWN CERTAINTY

Participants in Start the Conversation get a reading list on the very first night. And they get a little pep talk from me that runs something like this:

> *Someone asked me once whether I had 100 percent confidence that I would survive my own death— that is, my body's death. And I said—this was about six years ago—that I did, and moreover, that anything less wouldn't serve me at all when that in-*

evitable moment came. If I had even a .01 percent crack in my belief, which fear could squeeze through, then I would die terrified, just like most everyone else.

Dying terrified is an experience that I am completely unwilling to have. I don't suggest that you have it either. It's not a pretty picture. It's agonizing, in fact.

You can avoid this, and believe me, you want to. But to build the degree of conviction you're going to need and to get the gift of fearlessness that 100 percent certainty confers, and that all near-death experiencers have, you'll have to do some work.

Think hard along the lines we've been setting out, ask your toughest questions, express your doubts in concrete terms and open your mind wide. Empty yourself as much as you possibly can of the biases you grew up with, which probably surround you still.

It's useful to remember that you have, in your role as juror here, an obligation (to yourself, actually) to listen and to read with an open and unbiased mind. That's your assignment. Do it and a big victory is yours. You will see that the material we are presenting to you is coherent and logical. It makes a solid case.

Are you beginning to be convinced that survival is real? If you need to build your certainty about this (which you probably do), your best bet is to read as many firsthand accounts of near-death experiences as you can.

As you read, imagine that the person telling the

story is standing before you—a whole human being who has had a regular life (whatever that means) just like yours. Listen to his or her account, paying particular attention to those Sneaker on the Ledge details that are so important to our case. And then see what you think.

Here are some suggestions about movies to rent and watch as well. These are a lot of fun, and they make the same points we've been developing together.

SUGGESTED READINGS AND MOVIES

Life After Life—Raymond Moody
Closer to the Light—Melvin Morse
Saved by the Light—Dannion Brinkley

Resurrection—Ellen Burstyn
Ghost—Patrick Swayze, Demi Moore
Truly, Madly, Deeply—Alan Rickman

CHAPTER FIVE

THE SURVIVOR
JOURNEYS ON

W E HAVE SHOWN THAT some essence, some aspect, of a human being does operate beyond the body's physical boundaries, at least in those instances where the body is not heading toward permanent disintegration. To deepen our conviction that this is not an artifact of near-death versus full death, we really need to be able to track that survivor, whatever it may be, into the days and months and years following the body's demise.

Now when I say "track," obviously I am not implying that there is an unbroken trail we can follow the way we might follow footprints in the new snow. But our tracking of the survivor does have some parallels in the natural world. Think of how sophisticated biology has become. If a scientist wants to follow the migration of blue whales, for example, he or she will tag an individual whale with some sort of a transmitter and then follow the signals the transmitter emits. The whale itself may be out of sight for months at a time, but as long as some signal is received now and again, the scientist can be assured that the subject is out there somewhere.

In other words, the continued existence of the whale is not in question, ever. Moreover, even if the transmitter went dead, it could *not* be assumed that the whale had.

What happens when a person leaves the body for good—dies is what we usually say—is similar to what happens when the whale takes a deep dive and disappears from sight. The whale is in its element. We cannot follow. What keeps us from following along is *our physical limitation,* which the whale does not share. But we do allow that the whale still exists, because we get its weak little signal from time to time.

Now notice that where the survivor of the body's death is concerned, we are also unable to track it directly. Of course, it has not got a body anymore. It is out of *our* element. But remember, we are looking for faint signals, if you will, from that which is *not limited to the physical body,* in other words, from that which has some existence independent of the body.

Our long-standing belief that a human person is a physical thing keeps us from seeing the obvious here. Suppose you are out in the woods with binoculars, following the activity of a brilliant little cardinal. The bird ducks out of sight behind an especially large tree. You keep your binoculars trained on the tree because you know the bird will show up again—it has just passed from your sight temporarily. Just because you can't see it at the moment, you certainly don't assume that it no longer exists. There's just something big and solid—the tree, in this case—blocking your view right now.

OK, what blocks our view of the *actual* person when there is a dead body before us on the bed is that we think the person *was* that thing behind which it has just disappeared. We can tell easily that what had someone inside moments ago no longer does. The dead body is clearly some *thing* and not some *one.*

It's as if the tree has swallowed up the bird. So we keep

our gaze on the tree; after all, it's the last place we saw that bird. This is slightly embarrassing, but never mind. It's so understandable, this confusion of ours, because we've been relating to the person primarily through physical means, utilizing our body and theirs. Naturally, therefore, the association between the person and the corpse is pretty well embedded in our minds. It's not that different from the belief among certain so-called primitive peoples that a photograph, a merely physical representation of the person, can capture the person's essence and spirit it away.

Now, all we're hoping to find in our pursuit of proof that the person survives the body's demise is some evidence of personhood without the body. Beyond the near-death experience, we want to know if someone survives when the body has had a full-death experience.

My friend Diane said, "Oh, that's easy, Ganga, there are all those psychics, channelers, mediums. There's been so much written about this." I had to laugh. Of course, there's a huge amount of material out there and if that evidence is sufficient to build conviction *for you,* you really don't need this particular book.

The fact is that however credible the channeler or trance medium may be, most of us just don't take their efforts all that seriously. That's the truth. That matter of the *reliable* witness remains important. Most of us assume a person is not reliable if they haven't marched through our best universities, graduated from our best medical schools and stayed pretty well within the boundaries of, well, conventional wisdom.

I don't have an opinion about this one way or another. I just know from scrutinizing my own attitudes that this is so. I'm looking forward to the day when someone will be able to say, "I'm certain there is life after death. After all, my doctor said so."

That's why I keep bringing before you the published work of M.D. authors. As we all know, doctors are subjected to a rigorous training process that is firmly rooted in the logic of the scientific method. That training is also based on the assumption that a human being is limited to the body and therefore ceases to exist when the body dies. Within this tight intellectual framework, and for even the most open-minded and enquiring of physicians and medical students, the possibility of life after death cannot really be considered since, as we said earlier, it cannot be "scientifically" proved. And it defies the worldview on which medical studies are based.

With that much of a preamble, I must urge you to read *Many Lives, Many Masters,* by Brian Weiss, a Columbia- and Yale-trained M.D. psychiatrist. Not only does Weiss make a very solid case, way beyond all reasonable doubt, that we survive, but the book is also fascinating and great fun to read.

And imagine the reluctance, if you will, of a guy like Weiss to present his evidence—and evidence it is—that people do not die. The risk—let's say the certainty—of losing the respect of one's colleagues is no small matter for professionals who have worked so long and hard for that respect. Weiss said, "It took me four years to garner the courage to take the professional risk of revealing this unorthodox information."

So what happened to Dr. Weiss that was so compelling that he had to risk everything he had worked for and write it down? He tells his story in great detail in *Many Lives, Many Masters*. The gist of it is as follows:

Dr. Weiss had a patient named Catherine, who came for

treatment of some very unpleasant symptoms of intense anxiety. Despite the best methods of conventional psychother-
apy, Catherine did not improve. Weiss decided to resort to
hypnotherapy with her, on the assumption that her symptoms were probably rooted in some period of her life—early
childhood, perhaps—that she could not recall in a normal
waking state.

In her very first hypnotic trance, Catherine recalled two
events—one at three years of age and one at six—that
seemed to connect logically and causally to her present-
day symptoms. However, at her next appointment, she told
a baffled Dr. Weiss that her symptoms were absolutely
unimproved.

Weiss then led Catherine back into the hypnotic state and
gave her one simple clear command: "Go back to the time
from which your symptoms arise." What happened next
stunned Weiss enormously. For his patient began to relay details—very precise details and many of them—from a life in
which, almost four thousand years before, she had suddenly
drowned, swept up with her infant daughter in a tidal wave
that took out her whole village.

Not only had Dr. Weiss, of course, no prior belief in reincarnation, Catherine herself did not. But at their next session,
she reported joyfully that her lifelong fear of drowning and
the recurrent nightmares of drowning she had been suffering
had disappeared—permanently, it turned out.

That episode, the first of many excursions that Brian
Weiss and Catherine took into her past lives, launched the
young physician into an exploration of the medical literature
about reincarnation. He found, among other studies, the
carefully documented work of Dr. Ian Stevenson, a professor
of psychiatry at the University of Virginia, who reported over
two thousand examples of children with past-life memories,

many of whom were able to speak languages to which they had never in their present lifetimes been exposed.

Weiss remained naturally skeptical but worked along with Catherine steadily, perplexed that her symptoms continued to abate. He listened to what she reported, hoping, despite his long-standing professional bias against this, that she would offer some incontrovertible proof that what she saw and heard while under hypnosis was objectively, verifiably true.

And then it happened! At the close of a session, during which Catherine had recounted a death from illness long, long ago, she began to speak from a detached, impersonal between-incarnational state. And this is what she said:

> *Your father is here, and your son, who is a small child. Your father says you will know him because his name is Avrom and your daughter is named after him. Also his death was due to his heart. Your son's heart was also important, for it was backward, like a chicken's.*

What in these few words left Dr. Weiss absolutely convinced beyond any possible doubt of the truth of Catherine's reports? It was this:

1. *She had no prior knowledge whatsoever about his personal life.*

2. *His father, a robust sixty-one-year-old named Alvin, had died of a massive heart attack just a few years before. Alvin's Hebrew name, not recorded on any public documents, was Avrom. And Brian Weiss's*

daughter, born four months after her grandfather's death, was named Amy after him.

3. *The death at twenty-three days of Weiss's firstborn son had taken place eleven years before. The baby had been born with an impossibly deformed heart, which was, in effect, backward: the pulmonary veins with their essential oxygenated blood entered the heart on the wrong side. The baby could not have survived.*

For Weiss, this was the Sneaker on the Ledge—the evidence he could not deny or doubt that he and Catherine truly were exploring real lifetimes in the historical past. It was proof that, though she had many, many deaths, she had never ever ceased to be herself. She had never ever been annihilated. Only her many many bodies had died.

"And what"—he went on to say—"what about my father and my son? In a sense, they were still alive; they had never really died. They were talking to me, years after their burials, and proving it by providing specific, very secret information."

What do you think about that?

SUGGESTED READINGS

Many Lives, Many Masters—Brian Weiss, M.D.
Life Between Life—Joel Whitton, M.D., Ph.D.

CHAPTER SIX

THE SURVIVOR HERE AND NOW

We've tracked the one who survives death through the moments immediately following physical death, and we've caught glimpses of that survivor moving in and out of past lifetimes and even into the long pauses between lifetimes. But where is this survivor right now?

WHO IS READING THESE WORDS?

This is a critical part of our work together, so don't skip these pages, please. This is where we link the One who will survive your physical death with the person you are right this minute—reading these words. This is where the seeds of information and ideas are planted in the rich soil of daily experience so that they can take root there and bear the fruit we need, which is certainty that we are not extinguished at death. This is where real conviction—the sort that will give you peace and confidence at your own death—is built.

Here's the picture of the Premises of Annihilation and Associated Concepts again. Remind yourself that the foundation on which these premises rest is the notion that we are LIMITED TO these physical bodies.

What we're going to do now is spell out a few ways to

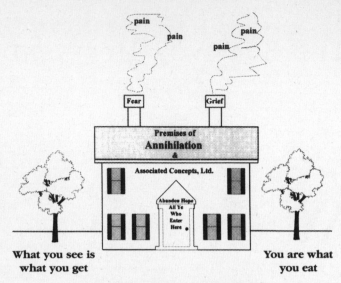

I Am Limited to This Body

catch a glimpse of the One who is not limited to these bodies, right here, right now.

By right now, what I mean is simply today. Let's look at a single twenty-four-hour period and see what our possibilities are in a single day.

AWAKE OR ASLEEP

Right now, we're both awake, I writing and you reading. This is called The Waking State. Later today, we'll both get sleepy and go to bed. Once we fall asleep, there are only two options: We'll either be dreaming or we'll be sleeping without dreams. Let's express those three possibilities this way:

There are just three major conditions, or states, if you will, available to us in a twenty-four-hour period:

The Waking State

The Dream State

The Deep Sleep State

Just as a near-death experiencer can watch what happens to the body while it is out cold, we can all watch what goes on when the body is working fine, when we are "alive and well." We do this without even noticing that we're watching and we do this all the time.

The One who watches, the one we call the survivor of the near-death experience, is the very same One who is alert and watching from inside our everyday skins all the time. Let's call this One the Witness, which works nicely with our earlier idea of a legal style of proof. The Witness is the One who sees and records it all. We're going to get to know the Witness of all three states, beginning with the Witness of The Waking State. Let me tell you a story.

THERE I AM

I had a friend some years ago, a very wealthy woman who was in her early nineties. One afternoon, she showed me a fragile old photo of herself as a little girl. "There I am," she said proudly, pointing to a luxuriously dressed little figure on the front seat of an elegant carriage. "My parents let me ride with the coachman—it was such a treat."

There was no physical resemblance at all between the little girl in the photo and the chipper old lady beside me on the couch in her cozy library. Yet Mrs. West had no trouble recognizing herself in the picture, though I would not have been able to pick her out.

She recognized herself in that very different body because she remembered the moment. She had witnessed it almost ninety years before, had held it for a moment in her mind's eye, recorded it and then called it up to share with me that sunny day, creating a magical bridge between her era and mine.

Who or what was it that captured the moment so long ago and that re-presented it that afternoon? It was the Witness of The Waking State. You can meet the Witness of The Waking State this very moment. It is the One who is reading these words on the page. Now close your eyes.

When you did that, the visual images disappeared. But notice that you were still fully present, aware of the sounds in the room and wondering perhaps whether any of these ideas makes any sense. The One aware of and watching your thoughts is also the Witness of The Waking State.

That One is not, emphatically not, the same thing as the mind. It is the Witness of The (Waking State) Mind. It's the One who, when you have a petty, nasty thought (or a sweet loving thought, for that matter) points it out to you, usually with a little scolding or praise folded in.

The One who observes your emotions is also the Witness of The Waking State. If you're not clear about what I mean, imagine this:

> *This evening, you call your best friend to relate a nasty encounter you had this morning on the way to work. You say, "I was so mad I could hardly speak. My whole day was ruined. I was so upset!"*

The One who vividly recalls the intense emotions of this morning is the Witness of The Waking State. That's not the one who got swept up and miserable (indeed, where is *she* right now?). It's the One who watched the encounter and can report about it without getting all upset again. It's the One who had some steady powers of observation, who was at a little emotional distance from the action. That's the Witness of The Waking State.

The Witness of The Waking State is most easily detected by calling up memories of childhood events.

Here's an exercise: Bring to mind any episode from your childhood, the earlier the better. Here's one of mine:

> *I can recall trying to build a house of playing cards on the floor of my Aunt Mary's apartment in Queens. The house would go up a few shaky, delicately balanced levels and then slip into collapse at a breath. I was very young—not quite two, Aunt Mary tells me. Naturally, I was in a much smaller body than I am now. My face was so close to the ground that the precariously built house of cards was indeed vulnerable to my breath. It collapsed again and again before I figured out what in fact the problem was.*
>
> *I can remember that my visual field was limited to the house of cards and a few squares of the parquet floor. Everything was big, especially Aunt Mary's face. The scale was very different and my memory is all visual, everything shot in close-up through the eyes of that child.*

OK, your turn. Pick, if you will, something you can recall in lots of detail—a holiday celebration, for example, a birthday, vacation or trip—something you can really recall the flavor of fully.

Now notice that the memory has two separate and quite

distinct components: let's call these the Picture and the Sound.

The Picture, like an old-fashioned home movie, was recorded at the only time it could have been, which was when the event took place. And the One who recorded it was the One who was there: the Witness of The Waking State, observing the events through the fairly naive eyes of that child—you.

Then there's the Sound. Say you are showing these old home movies to your present-day friends. And so you comment on the action and explain things as the film cranks along. There is laughter at such times because of that inherently funny gap between the way you looked and acted then and the way you are now.

Your commentary, the present-day voice-over, reflects your perspective as an adult: the point of view you have built on a mountain of little experiences like the ones in the movie. So the narrator, the one who has opinions, the commentator, tells the tale from the very different perspective of the person you are now. Now notice this.

Stop the action. Are you the same person whose cute little child's body was dancing on the screen? "Of course I am," comes the answer. "Can't you see?"

No, *we* can't see—and the reason we *can't* see is that your body is utterly different. The point of view from which you tell your story has changed as well, hasn't it?

But something stayed the same. What stayed the same is the One we call the Witness of The Waking State. The One who was watching then, in childhood, is watching now. The One who has ideas, opinions about what happened—that's the mind. The one the physical events or changes happen to—that's the body. But the one who watches the adventures of the body—and who listens to the opinions, ideas and feelings of the mind—that's the Witness of The Waking State and *that is who you actually are.*

This is such a subtle but critical point. Don't let it get away from you. Get up and walk to a mirror. See that face? Very different from the face you had as a little child, isn't it? But you are exactly who you always were, aren't you?

The One looking out through your eyes is the One who looked out through those eyes when your body was very young. The body has changed profoundly, but the One shooting the scenes that make up its ongoing movie, the eye of the camera itself, is the same, same, same.

That's why you can sometimes catch yourself thinking that it feels weird to be in this adult body, this aging body, when who you really are is the same as the kid you were, way back then. You might say, "Wow, I can't believe that's me!" when you catch your reflection in a store window or see a candid photo of yourself.

Of course, that's *not* you—that's just your body, your vehicle, your home. And the slight sense of disbelief you experience when you see that body makes sense because it lets you know that you're *aware* of being something steady and constant throughout and despite all the body's changes.

Remember we are tracking the one who is NOT LIMITED by the body. Do you see it yet? This life turns out to be a spectator sport. Go figure.

At the Reunion

I went to my thirty-fifth high school reunion last June (good grief!) and that was a nifty way to experience what stays the same and what changes. Every body is the same age, right, class of 1959. At the reunion, we were all fifty-three. What an interesting age.

Looking around the group, which seems to get smaller every time we meet, I saw that some of us had become grandparents and really look it. I had to peer hard at the faces to see if I could figure out who was hiding inside. And then some little sparkle of the high school classmate would break through and I'd recognize that people had remained who they always were, though they are now playing the role of proud grandparents, and playing it really well. And a few of us have stayed kids, somehow, despite having kids of our own. Immature is what we are and probably will remain. I haven't even changed my wardrobe much in all these years—still wearing chinos, sneakers, turtlenecks, sweaters and jeans. "Aging preppy" is what I call the look. I'm not trying to fool myself or anybody else either. I'm not trying to look younger. I just figure if it ain't broke, don't fix it. Comfort—that's what I need.

Anyway, here comes the cutest kid in the class, this guy named Izzy. Still the same guy, he's as playful and confident as ever. What's different is his body, of course, which is bigger around the middle and hasn't got quite as much hair on the top. The hair he has got is unnaturally black, but then, mine is unnaturally blond.

What's also different is that he's flirting with *me,* the former queen of high school shyness, in other words, one of the least popular girls in our class. I notice myself revert to being flustered and slightly undone, though I've been very sure of myself and not at all shy for lots of years. It's not because this is a serious flirtation either, as Izzy is married and I'm not available in any case.

But the fascination for both of us lies in the tension between the people we are now and the reanimated ghosts of who we were back then. Reunions are such a fascinating play because of this strange flickering dance between present and past, between figure and ground.

For our purposes here, what we want to point out is that the more it (the body) changes, the more it (the Witness of The Waking State) stays the same. The same kid who was intimidated by this quite popular guy thirty-five years ago is intimidated by him now—and also not—both at once. And just to blur the edges further, the One who noted and recorded that amusing moment at the reunion was the Witness of The Waking State. Got that?

The Witness of The Waking State registers all the mundane moments of our lives—even the minor events in our emotional, physical and intellectual development. When things are "business as usual," by which I mean that the changes in our feelings, our bodies and our ideas are taking place gradually, we don't notice the Witness much at all. But when the "fast forward" mode hits, that Witness is so much easier to detect.

WITNESSING BIG CHANGES

Shelly has been trying to get pregnant for as long as I've known her; that's about three years. She's getting into her late thirties and has been worried that she won't be able to have the child for which she and her husband yearn. I remind her that I had my daughter when I was forty-five, but of course, that's no comfort to Shelly. She wants to be pregnant now, not eight years from now.

When I saw her about six months ago, she had that "I've got a secret" face: big round eyes, subtle little smile. I waited for her to give me the news, wanting her to have the fun of choosing her moment and her words. She held out about thirty seconds. I tried my best to look surprised. "Oh, I'm so happy for you, Shelly!" And I was.

Then last week I ran into her in the neighborhood—we live a few blocks apart. And Shelly's body is BIG! Not fat— she had been a dancer, and was slender and fit from the get-go, but hugely pregnant. The baby—must be a nice big one—is due next month.

"How's it going, Shelly?"

"Great, Ganga, we're starting to believe we're getting a baby. But you know what? I don't feel any different—I mean, not at all. I can't sleep on my stomach, of course, and it's weird when I feel the baby move around—somebody else inside my body, how bizarre! But Ganga, I thought I'd feel like somebody else and I don't, I just don't. I'm still Shelly, I'm just the same. I'm not even pregnant in my dreams—isn't that weird?"

Because her body had changed so much and so fast, was so very different, albeit temporarily, from the one she'd been getting around in, Shelly was thrown into contact with the Witness of The Waking State. She had become aware of the One who is not the body but the observer of the body's transformations. "I'm still Shelly" was the way she put it. For our purposes, we'll translate that this way: "I realized I'm just the Witness of The Waking State."

And notice that she wasn't pregnant in her dreams—we'll come back to that point in just a little bit.

It was the huge change in her body that allowed Shelly to notice the Witness, the One she always was. (P.S. I found out today that she had a big baby boy.)

The Witness of The Waking State is so constant a presence in our lives that it's hard to stay aware of it—like the sound of traffic if we live beside a major road or that background music in the office.

But it's very important to learn to catch hold of and identify with the Witness of The Waking State because that changeless Witness is the One who makes it through the transition we call death.

Here are some tricks (techniques) to help you experience your self as the Witness of The Waking State. These are all easy and they are interesting to do.

He, She or Me

Normally most of us are very caught up in the ongoing drama that is our daily life—especially in these times when individual history is taken so terribly seriously. We tend to run an unbroken first-person mental or silent commentary about this most fascinating of individuals—I.

That monologue is the background noise in the mind. It may focus on the past, the present or the future. But the subject of this ongoing monologue is always I.

If, as an exercise in awareness, we substitute the appropriate third-person pronoun or our own first name, we get a very different take. Now watch this.

Imagine you have a choice seat in a comfortable theater. The play is a long-running hit and you are very interested in it because it's the ongoing drama based on your own life. Sitting front row center, watching the actor who plays you rush about onstage, you will notice that even though the action onstage looks very like what you went through earlier in the day, you now have no need to react. You are just watching.

If you comment at all on the action, you will use the third-person pronoun to describe the main character—the star. You may say something like this: "Oh, look what a big risk she's taking here" or "Why can't he see not to do that?"

All of a sudden the story concerns somebody else, some-body who, by definition, is not quite as important as "I" am. So you're detached, especially by contrast to the way you were when those events took place. All of a sudden you are seated in the audience, watching the exploits of an en-thralling character on the stage.

Because of your detachment, you're more aware of what the other characters in the play are up to. You're able to un-derstand your own character more clearly, too. You see a few more possible options than you did earlier in the day. You have distance on the action, in other words, and you have perspective. You gain strategically, enormously. You win.

Make good friends with the third-person pronoun as soon as you can. Shake off that stupefying I as much and as fast as possible. You'll see such interesting results. Note: The detached spectator is the Witness of The Waking State. That Witness is who you actually are.

Even if you were able to take my word for this, it would be insufficient. You'll need a direct experience of your own to really see what I'm talking about. And the easiest way to get that is to practice this simple technique. Practice it a lot.

Silently address yourself by your own first name or he or she. It's simple but it is not easy. The I (I am, I have, I feel) is so full of itself and so used to starring in your show. But the benefits of persevering in this practice are considerable. Here's one example of how this technique pays off.

Marilyn's Report. Marilyn has taken Start the Conversation a number of times now. She tells me it's the power of this little technique, applied diligently in her daily life, that keeps her coming back. Here's her story:

I work in the outpatient clinic of a large mental health facility. My desk is in a tiny cubicle along a very noisy corridor. It's a state-run facility and my job—I'm a psychologist by profession—is to separate out people who have real emergencies or who are dangerous to themselves from people whose problems are less extreme.

In any case, every single person I see all day long is in deep emotional trouble of some sort, so the stress in my work life is extremely high. And it carries over into the rest of my life. I get furious if someone crowds me in the subway, for example, which means I'm always furious—going and coming—and it takes me more than just an evening or a weekend to calm down.

The first couple of days I tried calling myself Marilyn instead of I, I didn't notice much change. I just felt a little weird. Then I began (and here she laughed and changed gears) then Marilyn began not to take each little hassle quite so seriously. She didn't feel like punching people on the subway— and she started laughing at some of the more extreme situations that came up during the day. My—her friends wanted to know if she was on Prozac or something. I—she feels so much better!

What makes this simple exercise so powerful? For most of us, the feelings that play through us in the course of a day are very compelling. That is to say, we take them *seriously.* We get swept up in these extremely transitory moods, feeling, I am furious, I am miserable, I am overjoyed, depressed, in love.

But if we get just a little distance on all this turbulent

emotional weather, we notice that it's the feelings themselves that are always and forever changing, endlessly arising and subsiding like the clouds in the sky outside our windows.

What's not changing? The One who's aware of these clouds isn't changing, just as the sky through which the clouds are moving isn't changing.

Getting that crucial distance from the emotional weather is what happens when we substitute the third-person pronoun or our own first name for that ever-captivating I.

You will not have a clue about the power of this practice if you don't try it out yourself. It will jump you right into the experience of your self as Witness. Give it a try. I mean more than once—for some weeks. You will see fascinating results.

Now here's another good one you can try. This is very interesting also—and fun.

The Headless One

This is another way to catch a glimpse of the One who's always watching. It's an exercise that is best used in those rare moments when there is no story line running in your mind. This is a technique for solitude, for a walk on the beach or in the woods, for the early morning hours, for a quiet time.

Take notice of the fact that you have no concrete experience of your body north of your shoulders. You can tuck your chin into the notch in your collarbone and see your chest and below. You can turn your head slightly and see the shoulders and arms. But unless you use a mirror, your head and neck are invisible. Unless you have a headache or your nose is stopped up, you can't really tell that your head and neck are there at all.

Walking by yourself, imagine that the physical boundaries of your head are gone. Float your awareness out as far as it will go. Distant sounds will drift into your hearing. Your field of vision will fuzz a little in the foreground but expand extraordinarily at the outer edge. (Please don't cross the street or drive in this condition.)

You've broken through the routine sense of where your boundaries are. Play with the experience that you are just your awareness, not the physical package at all. Imagine that you contain everything of which you are aware. It is all part of what you are. In point of fact, this is so.

MEDITATION

Perhaps you've been told by some well-meaning friend that you "should" meditate. If you're anything like me, that's probably been enough to keep you from exploring meditation at all. Something that's supposed to be good for you is not likely to be much fun—and besides, it's probably hard to learn and it's bound to be boring as well.

Wrong. And wrong again. Meditation is easy, as natural as breathing or sleeping and more likely than the average movie to be both interesting and fun. Moreover, it's another way to directly experience that you are the survivor, the spectator, the Witness of The Waking State.

There's another good reason to make friends with meditation, as Mary Ellen's story will show.

Just Two Regrets. Mary Ellen was one of the first participants in Start the Conversation, and the memory of her is as dear today as she herself was six years ago. She had a wide-open, friendly Irish face, wavy white hair, and an easy laugh. She also had quite a lot of cancer throughout her body. She had declined to continue with chemotherapy six months before we met but was being medicated fully and appropriately against pain.

Her doctors had said she had perhaps another three to

six months, and Mary Ellen was perfectly comfortable with that. She had lived her sixty-one years fully and had completed what she considered her life's work: the shepherding into adulthood of three fine kids.

As things went along, the tumor obstructed her digestive tract, and so Mary Ellen went into the hospital for what turned into a three-month stay, during which she was kept going by intravenous feeding, since there was no way she could digest food taken in by mouth.

It was an interesting situation—that's the way she described it. And that's what it was, because she looked wonderfully well, was in no particular discomfort and was in a kind of benign holding pattern, waiting for the cancer to make its move. She had absolutely no fear of death.

I asked her, on one of my visits, whether she had any messages, any teachings, to send back to the other students in the class, which was meeting weekly throughout this period. Oh yes, she said, she certainly did.

Mary Ellen had only two regrets, having lived so well and done so much of what she set out to do. And they were these:

1. *that she had ever walked past a Häagen-Dazs store without going in to get the ice cream she wanted, and*

2. *that she had never developed a meditation practice.*

Because she hadn't learned to meditate, she was trapped in the hospital bed with only a tiny black and white TV as respite from the relentless sameness of her days—and no ice cream either.

It makes such good sense to develop a meditation practice as a kind of insurance policy against being stuck as Mary

Ellen was, having no way out of a body that itself has no way out of the room—and because meditation is another way, along with the two techniques we have already described, to directly experience your familiar everyday self as the Witness of The Waking State.

Easy Meditation. Seat your self, your body, very comfortably. I like the living room couch around midday, when Hedley's off at school. Early morning is the classical time to meditate because it's easier to quiet down before the mind gets busy with the day. And those hours before and just after dawn are especially delicious—magical and still. But it's not always possible to get out of bed.

I find that being flexible about when I meditate has resulted in more frequent meditation than beating myself up over early mornings ever did. Whatever works for you.

If you're comfortable tucking your legs up under you, fine. But if they will ache and therefore distract you, just rest your feet flat on the floor. Be sure your back is well supported so that your sitting doesn't require any effort or strain. The idea is to park the body as securely as a car at the curb. That way you can lock it up, so to speak, and move away from it with ease.

I find that it pleases and comforts me to have a big, very soft pillow resting against my belly. Physical vulnerability, for me, seems centered in that area and if I cover it, then I can let go.

It's a good idea to unplug the phone or tuck it under a pillow, off the hook. You're getting yourself off the hook, too, and you don't want to be yanked back before you're ready. If I'm at all hungry, I have something light: a piece of toast, a little yogurt or applesauce, maybe some fruit. An empty stomach is best because you're less likely to be drowsy than after a meal. This is also not the moment for a cup of coffee or Irish breakfast tea—you're cranking down, not up.

Make sure there's nothing tight around your waist, so that you can relax the belly entirely and just let the whole body go. Usually, I wear clean sweatpants and a T-shirt, pull a soft mohair cap down over my eyes and drape a light shawl over my shoulders. In effect, I put the body into a cozy little cocoon so that it is warm and protected from drafts. Because it has no basis for complaint, I can take off. And I do.

What we're after here is a direct experience of the One who watches our waking state. And it's so easy. You will notice right off the bat that while your body is quite comfortable and still and your emotions are calm, your mind is racing around the room like a puppy or a two-year-old child. Do *not* be even slightly dismayed by this. Your awareness that the mind is a busy little bee is all we're after. That awareness IS meditation.

However, having said that, what you will notice next is that the busy mind is a demanding and tedious companion. The various concerns your mind is ceaselessly presenting are engaging, all right, very enticing indeed. Pretty soon you've hooked your caboose to whatever train of thought is running by.

You'll remember that there's a shopping list to draw up, a pressing phone call to make, urgent concern for someone you love, compelling business in the kitchen, dirty dishes, perhaps, or a book that has to go back to the library, now!

What you want to do in this case is just continue to watch. Remain amused. Notice the impulse to chase each thought. Picture the way a hyper puppy chases every single car, barking with full enthusiasm at each. That's about the way we chase our thoughts: we tear after each one until it disappears from sight. Right? Can we do something about this?

Since our aim is just to become familiar with the Witness of The Waking State, we've given ourselves a big head start by parking the body. Here's why.

At the Circus. The Waking State is just like a three-ring circus: in the center ring the parade of thoughts marches around. In one side ring is the emotional action, where the feelings do their ceaseless intricate dance, and in the other side ring, the body huffs and puffs about, making sure its endless requirements are met.

It's tough to stay aware of all that action simultaneously, just as it is at the circus. The minute you decide to focus on the amazing acrobats in the center ring, a troop of trained dogs starts doing some eye-catching stunts on horseback in one of the side rings. Your attention is drawn to that, then back to the center ring, then off to the other side. To say that your attention is scattered is seriously to understate the case.

Now, what happens when we sit to meditate is that the spotlights go out in those two side rings. The side rings are never really empty: stagehands are always clearing away the props from the last act and setting things up for the next one. But because those arenas are dark and because what's going on there isn't all that interesting, it's very much easier to be absorbed in the action in the center ring.

In the center ring plays the mind. Watching only that, we quickly notice our tendency to chase after each thought. Naturally—these are our own concerns and they are being presented in our own language, our own terms and our own voice. They must have some importance, right? There must be something we're supposed to do about them, right? Nope. Not right. Not right now.

On the Merry-Go-Round. There's a wonderful carousel in Central Park. It's just perfect. The music is loud and lively enough, the ride is long enough, the horses are big and bold and the price is right.

The controls are in the middle, the big lever that starts and stops the carousel is there, the sound system is there and the man who runs the whole show is there, too, just doing his job. Notice him starting the ride, hopping on, walking around to collect the tickets and nimbly hopping off again. Watch him ringing the big bell twice, as he did when we started up, and then pulling the lever that slows everything to a stop once more.

The cheery folk who have bought tickets, climbed on horses and ridden around are there to have some fun. But the operator of the carousel is working (yes, he may be having fun as well). Working means he doesn't go round and round as the carousel does, and he doesn't go up and down on one of the horses. He hops on to get his job done and then hops back off.

This is the ideal relationship between the Witness of The Waking State and the mind. The Witness watches the mind, with all its ingenious notions, go round and round. The Witness watches the moods, the feelings, go up and down like the horses—up and down, round and round. The operator of the carousel (that's the Witness) hops on when there is a job to be done, does the job efficiently and then hops back off. One experienced meditator described it this way: "My mind doesn't think unless I order it to." Imagine the freedom of that.

Remember, we're after an experience of ourselves as the Witness here. We're not interested, for our present purpose, in what the actual action is, either in the center ring or on the merry-go-round. Just noticing that the thoughts go round and round and the moods go up and down is all we're here to do.

Back to the operator of the merry-go-round. Perhaps he's new on the job and forgets from time to time that he's working. He jumps on a horse, goes up and down, round and round for a bit, and then, with some embarrassment, snaps out of it, collects the rest of the tickets, goes back to the center and sits down. And just watches.

What did the guy do to snap out of it? He reminded himself, *I am working.* In the same way, when your body is parked on the couch and you are hoping to enjoy a little peace but instead find your attention going round and round, up and down with the busy mind, you can remind yourself, *I am watching.*

The very best way to do this is to have that reminder running all the time. And the easiest way to have the reminder running all the time is to hook it up to something else that's running all the time—your breath.

So now you're sitting on your couch, breathing in and out. Every time you inhale, you hear *I am* like a whisper inside the breath itself. And as you exhale, *watching.* Want to make it even simpler? *I am* followed by *that*, meaning, "that which is *watching.*"

And now we're where we want to be. *I am that which watches. I am the observer. I am the Witness of all these thoughts. I am the Witness of The Waking State.*

Against this steady background of *I am that*, it becomes much easier to notice that a train of thought is rumbling through the station. Here's one more suggestion. If you want to improve your chances of not holding onto *any* train of thought but remaining as the relaxed, motionless Witness instead, try this.

Because the train of thought is made of words, we get

hooked up to it by a process of associating some words of our own with the phrases, clauses or sentences that are passing through. Say you are silently repeating *I am* with the in breath and *that* with the out breath. Now with *that* comes the thought *that library book is due* and with the next *I am* comes the thought *bored with this little exercise*. The words *I am that* are all in English, which makes it so easy to lose our vigilance and follow some other nice, easy, common English words down the track.

That's not even the problem. It's just as valuable to watch being drawn away from the center as it is to watch staying steady. Remember, we're interested in the act of watching, not in the contents of the scene. The problem is that we sometimes don't even notice being drawn away. One little string of English words seems just like any other; they are apples to apples. So off we go.

Here's a way around that. Put your *I am that* into a language that is nothing like your own—I'm going to suggest one—and you're home free because you will certainly notice when you lose focus and you will not be seduced into hopping onto any train of thought by similarities between and among the words.

So in Sanskrit, a suitably ancient and holy language, *I am that* is *Ham* (sounds like *hum*) on the in breath, and *Sa* on the out breath. No association to common English words is likely to trouble you now. What you've done, in effect, is move to a platform in the local station. The train of thought rattles through on the express track, if you will. And you sit quietly, comfortably, just breathing and watching, watching as the train of words-words-words-words-words just rolls on by.

By the way, meditation may give you quite a lot of peace and a strong sense of the basic "all-rightness" of your own nature. That's what near-death experiencers describe, too, when they speak of being aware that they are loved just as they are. It seems that the Witness is not the One who thinks you'd be all right with a little fine tuning or a major overhaul. The Witness knows that your life is a come-as-you-are party. And you're all right, right now.

THE WITNESS OF THE DREAM AND THE DEEP SLEEP STATES

What about the large part of this life we all spend sleeping? What does the Witness of the Waking State do when we are sleeping? Does it sleep too? Let's find out.

THE NIGHT WATCHMAN

Suppose you hired a night watchman to keep an eye on your country house. And suppose someone told you they heard a rumor that all these watchmen do is sleep—yours, too. So you call the watchman in and you ask him to prove that he wasn't sleeping.

"Easy," he says. "I saw those kids break the porch window just past midnight. I chased them off. And I heard the fire truck go by at quarter past five. Woke the whole neighborhood. And there was a long period between the kids and the fire truck with nothing whatsoever going on."

That little report is analogous to the report we all get but scarcely notice in the first few seconds after coming out of sleep in the morning. It runs something like this, in very abbreviated form: *dreamed—didn't dream.* If we're in the habit of paying attention to the report, it might be expanded to sound this way: *Very interesting dream—scary— exciting—strange—wonder what that was all about—maybe I need to write this one down . . . .*

Or this way: *What a deep sleep that was—up so late—no dream—nothing—boy, did I need that sleep* . . . .

Or, most typically, this way: *Slept like a log, just that one rambling bizarre dream I was in the middle of when the alarm went off* . . . .

Those reports are made by your own night watchman. And the watchman couldn't have been sleeping or he would have been unable to supply any detail at all about what went on in your dreams—or even that you dreamt at all, or—now this is fascinating—that you *didn't* dream.

Didn't dream means "nothing going on"—but the information that nothing was going on can only be brought to you by someone who stayed awake to *see* that nothing was going on.

That someone who stays awake and reports to us in the morning is what we call the Witness of The Dream and The Deep Sleep States—and that Witness, awake and alert without interruption all night long, is *who you are*.

THE SCREEN IS BLANK

This illustration is clearer still and it makes the One who watches all night long even easier to spot.

The room we use for Start the Conversation has a large video monitor in it with a VCR. From time to time, I do show a video to keep things lively and to illustrate some of the concepts of the course.

When we discuss the Witness of The Dream and The Deep Sleep States, I point out that the TV screen is blank. It's turned off. Then I recall the previous week's class, when we had a video to watch. "Does everybody see that the screen is dark right now, there's nothing showing? Right. But you have to be awake to know that, don't you? If you were asleep in your seat, you wouldn't be able to tell me what was up with the TV, would you?"

So in order to know that there was a period in the night during which you didn't dream, whoever let you know that would have to have stayed awake. And even to be aware that you did dream, whether you remember the activities of your dreams or not, you had to be watching. You had to be awake.

Tomorrow morning, just as you come out of sleep, notice that you get this little packet of information: *dreamed— didn't dream*. The one who gives you this routine news bulletin is you acting as your own night watchman, awake and on the job. That's the Witness of The Dream and The Deep Sleep States. You have no doubt concluded by now that it is the same as the Witness of The Waking State. Right you are.

Three Perfect Pearls on a Silken Thread. Here's a diagram to help you picture the ever-alert witness who is present and on the job throughout all three of your daily states.

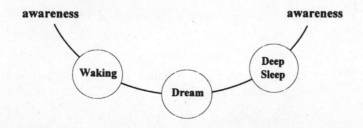

Think of this as a necklace of three perfect pearls. The thread that runs without interruption through all three pearls is your awareness, the watcher of all three states. And your awareness, that observer, the Witness, is *who you are*.

FURTHER ADVENTURES IN YOUR BED

Our night watchman's report proves the existence of the Witness of The Dream and The Deep Sleep States, but only after the fact, i.e., the first thing in the morning when we are already in The Waking State.

Is there a way directly to experience the Witness of The Dream State, to experience it *while* we're dreaming, so that we can become as familiar with it as we are with our Waking State Witness? There is.

Here's an exercise to try. Like everything else worth doing, it entails a little practice. But you're going to be sleeping and dreaming every night anyway, so there's plenty of opportunity to try this out. And once you get the hang of it, there's a fascinating new universe to explore.

Lucid Dreaming. Your goal is to realize, in the midst of a dream, that you are dreaming—in effect, to notice, while watching a dream, that you are in fact dreaming. There is a name for this condition of being "awake" while dreaming— it's called lucid dreaming.

The trick is to catch on that the events of the dream just couldn't be happening if you were awake. For example, you're on a date with John Kennedy, Jr., or Marilyn Monroe. You are flying. You are the president. (This is a nightmare.) You ask yourself, *Am I dreaming?*

Just noticing that you have asked yourself that question can tip you off to the fact that you *are* dreaming, since in The Waking State you never wonder if you are dreaming or not. Therefore, assume that if something makes you seriously wonder if you could be dreaming, you are.

For excellent suggestions on how to wake up while dreaming and how to explore and enjoy the dream state, pick up Malcolm Godwin's fascinating and beautifully illustrated book *The Lucid Dreamer*. And practice coming awake in your own dreams. Here's an example of the waking-up process.

Hedley's Lucid Dream. One Saturday morning—as usual we had slept late—Hedley came into my room to report a new experience. Here's an approximation of her account:

> *I was asleep at Auntie Elsa's house, in my room there, and Cookie (our energetic little dog) pooped on the rug. (This is no big deal at our house, but it's not something we want happening at Auntie Elsa's. In fact, if Cookie stays over there, she spends the night in the kitchen with her newspapers, her water and her food.)*
>
> *I was so upset about it that I woke up. Then I saw that I was still at Auntie Elsa's house and not at home. So I knew I must still be dreaming. So I woke myself up for real and I was in my own bed. That Cookie, she had pooped on the rug. Will you take care of it please, Mom?*

Notice that it was the reality check that Hedley ran—"I was still at Auntie Elsa's, not at home"—that made her realize she was in a dream. When the Witness of The Dream State becomes aware of itself, a distinction has been discovered between the star of the dream, the one who's playing the lead, and the one watching the dream go by. Very handy. Very nice. That's just what happens when you get the Witness of The Waking State in place. You pull back from the one it's all happening to just enough to watch what's happening.

Even an occasional lucid dream will reveal the one thing we are interested in for our study of death and survival: that the Witness of our dreams is identical to the Witness of our waking state and our deep sleep state through all the years of our lives. And that Witness—the survivor—the One who sails through death and out the other side—is *who you are.*

Have you got that?

SUGGESTED BOOKS AND MOVIES

The Lucid Dreamer—Malcolm Godwin
Alice's Adventures in Wonderland—Lewis Carroll
Through the Looking Glass—Lewis Carroll

Groundhog Day—Bill Murray
My Life—Michael Keaton

CHAPTER SEVEN

THEN WHAT DIES? AND HOW DOES IT DIE? AND DOES DYING HAVE TO HURT?

I F, AT THIS POINT, you haven't developed some conviction, some substantial conviction, that you are not limited to the body and that you will not die when it does, then let me suggest that you read the rest of what follows "as if" you had. And don't get too impatient. Don't beat yourself up. You can get it if you really want it. Persevere.

Remember that it took me eleven years of intense grief after my mother died and then nineteen more years of thinking about and reading about death to put these little pieces of information together into one coherent picture. One of my early students, Donald, who's very bright, had an "Aha, I see now" after coming to class over and over again for a year. So look, we're working to unplug a very deeply entrenched misconception (the Annihilation Premise), and that might take some time. Meanwhile, let's keep going.

WHAT DIES?

It's only the body that dies. Most of us have just one primary concern when we think about that moment of actual separation from the body. It boils down to this: Is it going to hurt? If so, will the pain be more than I can bear?

Let's tackle the matter of pain associated with death. There are only three possible ways that death can come to the body. Death can come:

1. *suddenly*

2. *gradually through asphyxiation over a (short) period of time*

3. *slowly over many days, weeks or months*

Let's take a broad general view of each of these possibilities, one by one.

SUDDEN DEATH

Instantaneous death is painless by its very nature, since the body's ability to register pain is immediately eliminated. Anyone who has ever fainted or been knocked unconscious knows that there is no pain involved. So sudden death is something no one should ever fear—from the standpoint of pain. Will it hurt? No. It can't.

Death as a result of sudden grievous injury, as in a car accident, stabbing or shooting, death that may take a few minutes to come about, is always eased enormously by the body's automatic release of natural painkillers—endorphins—into the bloodstream. There's an excellent discussion of this phenomenon, with examples drawn from both personal experience and his own medical practice, in Sherwin Nuland's book, *How We Die*.

The chapter in which Nuland discusses this is called "Murder and Serenity." As he makes clear with numerous examples, there is an obvious calm in people who have been suddenly and profoundly hurt. That calm lets us know that whatever experience (shock, disbelief, dissociation) the person is having, it is certainly not the awful agony about which you and I naturally worry. It is not possible to be both tranquil and in terrible pain unless we are anesthetized by our own body's mechanisms. And we always are.

A Small Story

I had an experience of this natural painkiller when I was living at home for my senior year in high school. I had gotten into one of those fierce power struggles with my sister that characterized our relationship all through the childhood years. I'll spare you the details, but what it came down to was that when the shouting match grew loud enough, our mother emerged from her room, and with a single sentence, decided the dispute in Elsa's favor. How hard could it be to choose practicing the piano over watching TV anyway? Easy shot. Piano wins.

I stormed into my room, furious at the injustice of it all. Just to demonstrate my point of view, I slammed the bedroom door as hard as I could—a very teenaged thing to do. The force of that grand slam whirled me around to face the door, so I was right in position when the top two-thirds of the full-length mirror—alas, no longer mounted on the door—came down like a guillotine on my left knee. Whoops.

The moment is still so vivid. I looked down to see what reminded me at the time of one of those excellent drawings in the *National Geographic*—you know, the kind that shows the layers of the Earth's crust all neatly differentiated. I remember noting skin, muscle, yes, yes that must be bone, and then instantaneously a great lake of blood on the floor. I heard myself scream, watched myself reach down for the lower leg with both hands—as if I thought it might fall off, which I did—and holding onto that leg, hop backward to my bed, and sit down.

Now there was no pain of any kind, and we're talking about one mighty deep cut. It wasn't until many hours later, when I woke up in the recovery room after surgery, that I had heavy-duty pain. And then I had it for several weeks; painkillers didn't eliminate it either. It took weeks to ease up.

But what spared me during the first several hours was the natural anesthesia that kicks in if we're injured like that. Think about it: The purpose of pain is to let us know that something needs to be taken care of immediately, that something is amiss.

But if the wound is major and beyond repair—in other words, if we're going to die of it—then the pain would be pointless, wouldn't it? It would just add insult to injury; what would be the gain? What genius designed these bodies?

GRADUAL DEATH

Gradual death, death that comes in a few minutes to a few hours because of insufficient oxygen in the blood, is the second of three possibilities. And here, too, we can be reassured where the matter of pain is concerned by some experiences many of us are familiar with.

People who have been revived after nearly drowning report that the sensation while their lungs were filled with water was one of peace, not pain. A student in Start the Conversation who nearly drowned in childhood said it was so blissful that after the lifeguards revived him, he tried to get back into the pool.

Most of us haven't come close to drowning. But the almost universal experience of becoming drowsy in a poorly ventilated room (remember classrooms in winter in elementary school?) lets us know that drowsiness—a sort of stupefaction—is what comes about when the brain doesn't get enough oxygen to function.

You can find numerous examples in your own life of what it feels like to gradually not be getting quite enough oxygen. You lose focus, can't pay attention, can't seem to stay awake. Unless there is a reason you *have* to stay awake (you're driving, for one), the surrender to sleep is quite delicious. Notice that if you get fuzzy when you're driving and can't stop for a break, you will automatically open the window and get some fresh air.

If you visit a friend who is near death, that person may be getting oxygen through nasal tubes or a face mask. She or he will be drowsy and weak, no doubt, but these are not painful conditions.

However, fear of death, which floods so many people at the last possible minute, can make even a frail drowsy person agitated and panic-stricken. This is very real pain, to be sure, but it is mental, not physical. It is based on the Annihilation Premise, which, as you recall, is incorrect. Indeed, it is this awful fear at the end that we are working together to remove, for ourselves and for everyone who will die.

DEATH AFTER PROLONGED ILLNESS

So the question of physical pain arises only when death comes gradually, as a result of a chronic illness. And here there is very good news to report. There is now a medical specialty called pain management, which trains doctors to have really in-depth knowledge of and respect for the problem of pain.

PAIN MANAGEMENT

The technology of pain control, especially the knowledge that certain combinations of drugs can virtually eliminate pain, leaving the patient both comfortable and alert, has come a long way in the past decades. What hasn't changed as much as it must is the philosophy of pain management.

At the core of the problem of insufficient pain control is an imbalance in the doctor-patient relationship. And this is not just the doctor's fault. Most of us would still like to be the passive partner in our own health care. We figure the doctor has the answers and should make our choices for us.

This approach blows up in our faces if we wind up in acute or chronic pain and locked into a relationship with a physician who undermedicates. Remember, your doctor isn't feeling your pain—there's a limit to how much real grasp of your situation his empathy for you can provide him. And everyone has a different tolerance of physical pain. So that makes it your job to communicate clearly and accurately what's going on with you and what you want done about it.

Now here's the bad news: The most common form of drug abuse in the late stages of painful illness is the under- (not over-) utilization of pain medication. And recent studies have demonstrated that there's a puritanical streak in many Americans, which shows up as not taking prescribed painkillers on the schedule the doctor recommends, or not accurately reporting the intensity of the pain. What on earth makes us ashamed to admit we're in pain? Or makes us believe that we don't deserve complete relief, if relief is possible?

If you recognize yourself in the last two sentences, I suggest you get a grip. Pain is rotten for morale, it puts us in a lousy mood every time, and it even keeps the body from doing whatever repairs it can in a timely manner. The body experiences pain as a source of stress, so it marshals its forces to deal with stress, not to repair damaged tissues through rest. It cannot rest when there's intense pain.

Moreover, the sight of you in pain is bound to be excruciating for people who love you. If pain as a part of chronic terminal illness is what we're talking about, why would you suffer any at all if it were preventable?

Now I realize you may feel differently about this, but I have to put my bias against physical pain up front anyway. When we speak of people who are "long-suffering" (is this too old-fashioned for you?) we mean people who put up with something fairly unpleasant for a long time. But we're not talking about putting up with the kind of pain that makes us sweat, pant and squirm. What would be the point?

Only in childbirth is there a reason to minimize the use of medications, and that's because another human being's welfare is involved. And because the pain (don't call it "discomfort" around me) of labor is intermittent, not constant, and because the whole process should be done in under a day, there might be a case for toughing it out. I personally can't imagine what that case would be, though, and my second baby was delivered by Caesarean. Otherwise, no deal.

I know, I know, there are risks to Caesarean section, too. And there are certainly women for whom giving birth is no big deal. But I'm not one of them. As far as my narrow little body was concerned, there was nothing natural about it at all.

I've never known anyone who got nicer, sweeter, more available to give and receive love when they were in a lot of physical pain. Have you? So if you've been unwilling to accept sufficient medication or afraid to insist on it, in other words, if the person to blame for inadequate pain control is you and not your doctor, get over it.

And by the way, that goes for emotional pain as well. There's no more of a moral victory to be had by toughing out emotional pain than by doing some stiff upper lip number in the face of physical pain. Depression, anxiety and all their kin can be sent packing, if not done in entirely, through the proper medications. People who are predisposed by their ancestry (Scandinavians, for example) to be more susceptible to depression than the average person (as I am) would do well to take note of this.

One of the most pernicious things about mental or emotional pain is that whereas physical pain, when it's severe enough, forces us to seek some kind of relief, emotional pain tends to move us in the opposite direction. Have you noticed this?

Physical pain provides the energy to find a way out, and fast. It compels us to. Who holds the hot potato in her hand, wondering what it reveals about her character if she lets it drop? Or wondering whether she deserves the relief that will come when she drops it? No one. Not ever. But these inappropriate considerations sometimes stop us from getting medical relief of emotional pain. They stopped me for years and years. How sad and foolish to suffer unnecessarily. I don't anymore and I never will again.

If, however, it's your doctor who's the problem and not your stubborn pride, there is a lot that you, as a health care consumer, can do to shield yourself from unnecessary pain.

Ask your physician up front what his or her philosophy of pain management is. Some doctors still believe that there's a problem with drug addiction when the opiates are prescribed. If you are in the last six months of a painful illness, there can be no concern with addiction. If your present doctor does not wholeheartedly support your wish to be as pain-free as possible, hire someone who does.

How John Got His Way

John Roth was a quiet, fairly shy young Oklahoma man who had AIDS. He'd been coming to the ongoing Conversation for over three years, and he never dwelt on—never even mentioned, for that matter—the many things that had gone wrong with his body—including the fact that he was gradually going blind.

John endeared himself to everyone in the group by his enormous courage—there is really no other word—and his utter lack of self-pity or self-dramatization. John had guts. John had heart. But John had no stomach whatsoever for physical pain. But off and on over the years, he had to have a number of pretty painful procedures done. We always encouraged John to insist on adequate pain medication whenever he had to have something difficult done. And John got quite good at this. Here's John's approach.

Before the procedure, he let the doctor know that he expected to be medicated for pain *in advance*. If the doctor tried to start work on John before the medication took effect, John would refuse to let him proceed. John fussed. He joked. He threatened to scream and kick (always with a smile on his face). But nobody ever thought John was kidding.

Two summers ago, John was in Santa Fe on vacation and had to be admitted to the hospital on the very first day because of a high fever. The infection causing the fever was traced to his Hickman catheter, which is a tube that goes into the body at the chest and stays in place, allowing medications to be administered without the nurse struggling to find fresh veins each time.

The Hickman is quite common among people who have

been living with AIDS for some years and need an array of medications daily. This was John's situation. When the Hickman's in place, it's not troublesome, except if infection develops. But having one removed can be painful and John's Hickman had to come out. I spoke with him long-distance two days afterward, and this was his high-spirited, upbeat report:

> *Well, I told them to wait until the pain stuff kicked in, but they didn't, so it hurt a lot—and I cried and cried. They said it was only five minutes, but five minutes is a hell of a long time if you're hurting. They weren't hurting at all. I was.*
>
> *Next morning when they came to check on me, I really let them know. I told them they better never try a stunt like that again. I told them they wouldn't have done it that way to their own sons. I really rubbed it in. I don't think they'll ever be so callous with anyone again.*

John had learned how to make sure that nobody disregarded his wishes—not more than once, at any rate. But the point here is that these understandings are best arrived at before the fact—when you can meet your doctor calmly and with strength, in other words, when you're not hurting. Know that the doctor is your employee and you *can* have it the way you want it. You're the boss.

When it comes to your death (life as well, obviously), it's your show. So if you have a question about whether it has to hurt, remember that it *doesn't* have to. But the key to a pain-free transition lies in the relationship you build with your doctor. This is urgent business. Build it now.

RECOMMENDED READING

Susan S. Lang and Richard B. Patt, *You Don't Have to Suffer,* Oxford University Press, 1994.

This is the best and most thorough book on this topic that I have seen, or can imagine, for that matter. The authors, one a physician, the other a science writer, have an extraordinarily helpful chapter called "On Being an Active Health-Care Consumer" that has headings like these:

What to Expect from Doctors

What to Look for in a Doctor

Checklist for Choosing a Doctor for Pain Management

When the Doctor Does not Take Pain Seriously

Accept Nothing Less than Satisfactory Relief

The authors have taken the trouble to describe everything that works to relieve pain—not just medications, but acupuncture, hypnosis and various physical therapies, as well as meditation, biofeedback and surgical intervention.

The most important thing, in my view, is that they take pain seriously and offer a wide-range array of information in completely accessible language about how to find relief. While the focus is on cancer pain in particular and the uncomfortable symptoms that may arise during cancer treatment, their information is universally useful. Get this book. And hang onto it.

About the Body

And by the way . . . about the body. Have you noticed how much work it is to maintain? Of course, while it's a sweet young thing, we don't mind at all. We're marketing the thing, so it's got to look good. It's possible to have a pretty good time in the body, especially while it is young, healthy and strong, that's for sure.

But here's the real deal. Every single thing the body produces has to be disposed of right away. Yes, there is one exception: A woman's body can produce a baby. But what's the first thing you do with a new baby after you dry it off? Diaper it. If you want inside information on the body, a friend of mine suggested this: Stick a finger into any one of the body's orifices. Take the finger out. Smell it. Got the point?

The only thing the body puts out on a regular basis is so stinky that we have to get rid of it right away. And there's no market for it either unless you're a horse or a cow. So the body is a shit factory—that's the bottom line. And we can't even give the stuff away, much less sell it. Wonderful.

How seriously do we take this marvel of efficiency, this wonder that can turn the most sublime dinner into smelly garbage in just a few hours? Ever watch people working out at the gym? This is very funny: the effort, the struggle, the gravity, the sweating and grunting. I do it, too.

Here we all are polishing up something that has no future, literally, and that will be a public health hazard the minute its owner lets it go. We even have to hire specialists in hazardous waste to undertake to dispose of it. And that's true no matter how young and pretty or pumped up and sleek the body was before its inhabitant split. This is not to imply that the body has no value, or shouldn't be well maintained. But here's how confused we can get.

THE BODY IS HOME

Twenty-three years ago, I was the happy tenant of an especially beautiful apartment. The high ceilings, hardwood floors and flawless moldings were all superb. But best of all were the light and the view: sunshine flooding all six rooms, the Hudson River in all its marvelous moods visible from every window and no other buildings near enough to require that we pull the shades down ever.

In fact my neighbor to the south was the old Trinity Parish Intercession Chapel Cemetery, with its stately trees and dignified ironwork gates. I really loved living there.

Anyone coming into my home felt happy to be there, too; it was just a lovely space. So I entertained a lot: brunch every Sunday, neighbors dropping in, food always being served. I noticed that if people met me in some other setting, I was quick to invite them home. I believed that if they hadn't seen my apartment, they wouldn't have any idea who I was.

I, of course, didn't have any idea who I was. I thought I was an apartment! A rented apartment, at that. Can you guess what I went through when it was time to move?

UP IN THE GROSS LAB

I got some close-up looks at the body, from a fairly bizarre perspective, when I was in my early twenties. Here's what happened:

I had dropped out of college for the first time about a year before the phrase "drop out" came into the language. Naturally my parents were dismayed by this. Furious is what they actually were.

So I did what my dog does when she's pooped on the rug—she hides under the bed. *I* hid out in a midwestern city about a thousand miles from home. Long-distance phone calls were not as routine then as they are now, and I knew I wouldn't have to deal with more than one tirade a month, given the cost of the phone call. Anyway, I couldn't afford to put in a phone.

The job I wound up in, after a stint as a nurse's aide, was as lab technician in the anatomy department of a university-affiliated medical school. And no, I had no qualifications for that or any other job, but was hired as a trainee. In truth, I could hardly manage that.

The first thing I noticed—this was in September of 1961—was a penetrating, unfamiliar but not unpleasant odor that permeated the top two floors of the building where I worked. "What is that smell?" I asked my boss.

"Oh, that's just the gross lab—no big deal, you won't even notice it by next week," said the boss.

Not wanting to make it obvious that I had no clue what the gross lab was, I headed up there on a lunch break. You must know what I saw. There were the first-year medical students hunched over their cadavers, two students per cadaver. How the sight of forty greasy gray plastic cadaver bags, their industrial-strength zippers running straight down the middle, head to foot, stunned and scared me that first day.

I was a literature major in college. I had never even pithed a frog. I was definitely not prepared for forty human bodies zipped into bags, being carved up by all these earnest-looking young guys—and it was guys, in those days.

But curiosity prevailed. I came cautiously into the room. Here's what I saw: Whatever was in those body bags was in no sense a human being anymore. What had been the flesh was grayish, puckered and oily. There was no blood, nothing particularly smelly or messy, no fluids that seemed at all familiar, no sense that there had been any particular person associated with these remains. There was nothing, after all, to be averse to or horrified by, and I could see that right away. The sense of there being anything creepy or untoward about this setting dissipated immediately. No problem. Nobody home.

Later I learned that the bodies in the dissecting lab are soaked a year (I wonder if it's still done this way) in formalin, a preservative, before being brought before the students. The veins and arteries are injected with red and blue plastic to allow the students to trace their paths more easily.

Certainly anyone who offers their remains to be used as a teaching tool in this way is making a significant gift. I can't imagine that a medical student could get the same intimate knowledge of what goes where by peering at a diagram, can you? And we have no other use for this body thing once we've moved out. As I said, we even have to pay someone to dispose of it. That's the bottom line.

My point is simply that there was no way to confuse those greasy remains with anything as subtle and refined as a human being. I wasn't consciously, at least in those days, struggling to understand the relation between the body and its occupant, but in this medical school setting, some bizarre experiences were coming my way, and I was learning a lot.

UP ON THE ROOF

Spring came around, and my friend David and I used to hang out from time to time on the roof, me smoking cigarettes (well it was 1962, what did we know?) and David, a seriously ambitious premed student, obsessing about his career. What a good-hearted guy he was, but driven. He did go on to do wonderful things.

Now the roof was one floor above the dissecting lab, the smells from which were a little more intense with the warm weather. The medical students had made mincemeat, so to speak, of their cadavers, though there were still major items left behind in those bags: bones, for example, skulls included. What to do with these?

Forgive me, but as I recall this I can't help thinking of what's left of the turkey a week after Thanksgiving. (Have I lost you yet?) It's the carcass, right, the meat is all gone. Your mom will make soup if she's a soup-making mom. Otherwise, out it goes. So what about these human remains? Soup makings they're not.

On one end of the roof was a crude little shed. In and out of the shed, which had tar paper on the outside, as I recall it, went a fellow named James. James was the diener, David said. What is the diener, I wanted to know. Well, he does the jobs nobody else does around the anatomy department—pathology too. David was being vague. I walked over to the shed to see for myself.

James the diener was an orderly guy. There was an incinerator in the shed. In one corner of the shed were arms and leg bones, torsos in another corner, heads against the far wall. James was feeding the individual pieces into the fire. Whew.

There was a pint bottle of something helpful, I mean booze, in his back pocket. James was sweating, working steadily and with concentration, mopping the runoff from his forehead with his shirtsleeve, working on.

Oh, boy, oh, boy. I walked back over to David, who smiled and shrugged. He was a science type. No big deal for him.

But what am I doing here? I remember thinking. *This is too bizarre—why am I seeing these things? I'm twenty-one years old, I'm a writer. Why should a twenty-one-year-old would-be writer have to think about death?*

Of course, I didn't know that my mother's death was just three years away. But as I set these words down on a peaceful sunny Sunday morning, my own precious daughter sweetly asleep in her room, I remember the first person I brought a God's Love We Deliver meal to on a February afternoon in 1986. He was twenty-six years old, but as bent and weak and wasted as a ninety-year-old man. His name was Ben and he said to me, so touchingly, "Why should a twenty-six-year-old man have to think about death?"

It was a heartbreaking question, especially from a boy whose father had said he could come home to North Carolina, but only if he came home in a box.

Nonetheless, the answer to Ben's sobering question remains—why not?

Seeing those stacks of parts in the incinerator shed so many years ago added another layer of experience to the conviction that was beginning to build in my mind: Whatever the mysterious human person is, it is not a collection of body parts, thighs, breasts and drumsticks. We are not the same as a Perdue chicken. We are not.

DOWN IN THE MORGUE

What next? My boss dispatched me across the street to the pathology department to learn the trade of the histology technician. In other words, she sent me to the autopsy lab. The autopsy lab was where the specimens gathered at autopsy were processed so they could be examined under a microscope and analyzed. This is a very ingenious process, the details of which I'll spare you for now.

Suffice it to say that I was working right next to the autopsy room itself, with all its astonishing sights, sounds—yes, and smells—an Alice-in-Wonderland world, in which every-thing was getting curiouser and curiouser.

The body to be autopsied would be brought up from the basement coolers on a coffin-shaped elevator—more a dumbwaiter, really, as it ran on a creaky antique pulley hauled up on frayed old ropes that had to be pulled by hand. The platform itself was just some crude planks nailed to-gether, wide enough for the corpse.

How did we know there was about to be a "post"? The elevator would begin to wail as James the diener hauled it up. *Wee-ohh, wee-ohh, wee-ohh, wee-ohh,* it would cry, as the rope and the pulley together sang their lamentation over whoever it was—had been—on the planks. It was almost too perfect a sound effect, as if some kid's horror movie were running in the other room.

Then would come the smells five or ten minutes later. These were especially rough around lunchtime. None of us ever tried to eat in the lab—obviously. Still, it was hard if you had just come back from the cafeteria. This was bath-room odor—but intensified to an amazing extent and with an overlay of fresh blood that was quite unnerving.

Mercifully, the ventilation system was efficient and noth-ing ever stayed in the air for long. Still, this would happen three or four times on some days, and we never knew ex-actly when until the dumbwaiter began its cries.

At first my coworkers laughed at me. I was so squeamish and they were such a cheerful lot. They were laughing con-stantly at and with one another and especially at me as I struggled to get my gag reflex under control. Eventually, the same impulse that walked me into the gross lab across the street drew me into the autopsy room. I was curious to see what I'd been smelling. Here's what I saw: There were four shiny stainless steel tables—each slanted about five degrees from head end to foot, each with a deep sink, with oversized drain and long hose at the lower end. There were grooves running the length of each table to channel runoff from the body (blood, etc.) into the sink. A white enamel pan scale hung at the sink end of each table. *Well and efficiently designed,* I remember thinking at the time.

Floors and walls were tiled so everything could be hosed down, and there were drains in the floor—gleaming stainless steel sinks against one wall—and tables against another where specimens could be trimmed and dropped into bottles of preservative for processing. The room was kept chilly, naturally, and had an eerie cleanliness about it. There was too much disinfectant in the air; it was hard to breathe normally. This was between autopsies, of course. During autopsies I endeavored not to breathe at all.

The passageway between our lab and the autopsy room was where James the diener hung out between jobs, sleeping in a rickety wooden chair that he propped at an angle against the wall. The walls of this dark little passageway curved as they ran along between the two rooms. They were lined with shelves—very dusty wooden shelves that held old-fashioned gray stoneware crocks—large crocks, they were, on the right side, and mason jars with murky liquid in them on the left.

And in the murky liquid, packed in with almost no leftover space, was "stuff," unidentifiable stuff, that looked something like the pigs' feet in a jar you can sometimes see at a deli.

What on earth could any of this stuff have to do with the buoyant and holy spirit of a human person? This was just some pickled garbage. Just remains. So much for the precious corpse.

CHAPTER EIGHT

REVISITING FEAR AND GRIEF

FEAR FIRST—FEAR IS THE WORST

Imagine walking along a jungle path in the twilight and hearing a lion roar. Your skin turns clammy, a knot forms in your stomach and you can taste the fear rising in your throat. Now imagine walking along a zoo path at the same time of the evening and hearing the same sound. This time you do not feel afraid.

This is the first paragraph of a fascinating article by Sandra Blakeslee that ran in the science section of the *New York Times* on December 6, 1994. Drop by the library if you'd like to read the whole thing. Here's the piece of our puzzle that this recent research sets in place.

Fear is permanently ingrained in the brain. The circuits, the networks of nerve cells in the brain that enable us to get scared and flee are just about the same as they were back when everybody had to run from roaring lions all the time.

That circuitry, which is hardware and not software, so to speak, has kept our vulnerable but smart species around for eons. That biological mechanism has been "highly conserved through evolution," and a good thing it has, too, since without it all our ancestors would have been cat food.

However, things have changed, and we know that if we hear a roaring lion these days, it is most unlikely to represent possible harm. We don't even *feel* afraid. We certainly don't sprint down the zoo walk in terror. That's because something we *know*—that there are no loose lions in San Diego, St. Louis or The Bronx—has modified our response on a very deep level. We no longer experience the fear.

There are mechanisms in the brain to inhibit inappropriate reactions. So our instinctive response—fear—gets adjusted to reflect the truth of the matter. The message that lions are dangerous gets modified by the zoo idea (in the frontal region of the brain) and we don't experience the fear at all. Good news. In fact, great news!

It has been my strong hope that if I can convey to you that death is not a wipeout, if you become convinced of this, as near-death experiencers are, then the terror you might otherwise feel when facing your own death would simply go away. I have been praying that this would be the case—that knowledge could transform experience somehow—that we could LEARN not to be afraid.

Courage, whatever it is that lets us go forward despite our fear, is like any other attribute: some of us have it and some of us never will. But anyone can acquire information, right? And with the right information, we don't *need* courage; we are simply not afraid.

HOW THIS WORKS

Suppose you understand, I mean really KNOW, that your inevitable exit from the body will be experienced as a blissful and deeply peaceful transition. Suppose you know you will *survive*. Ask yourself what would become of your fear of death. It would have to disappear, wouldn't it? Let me give you an example of what that might be like.

A LITTLE TEST

One July afternoon in 1987, I dropped in at the eyeglass store on the ground floor of my apartment building on Broadway and 83rd Street in New York City. My errand was to see whether some glasses my friend Costa had ordered were ready to be picked up. There were no other customers in the store—an unusual condition for which I was grateful.

The clerk, a tall young Indian woman, stood behind the cash register, just inside the door. I asked whether the glasses were ready—she took a step or two away from the register to look up Costa's name when in the door came a young, sickly-looking man who was not at all the usual customer for this fairly pricey store.

He wore a dirty vest-style undershirt, a pair of stained chinos, and his hair was longish, stringy, dirty. There was an ominous-looking shiny yellow plastic bag over his right hand and wrist, which shook slightly. Not a good sign.

He addressed two questions to me as if I were the clerk. "How much are these glasses here? You selling them?" Then he slid the yellow plastic bag off his hand.

And here was a very large gun. Not a little Saturday-night special—this was the sort of weapon, if my experience at detective movies serves, that takes out large sections of the body, leaving nothing usable behind.

Well, I had no moves to make, really. He was between me and the door. So there we all were—the clerk, the man with the gun and I. This had just become the last afternoon of my life.

I stood there, empty and still. Time had frozen. The clerk

screamed, a loud, almost comically theatrical scream, mouth wide open, arms over her head, fingers spread.

Then she ran, ever so slowly, it seemed, to the back of the store, along the narrow passageway behind the counter. I watched her run, fascinated, detached—fully expecting the middle of her back, which seemed such a broad and easy target, to blossom into blood.

I had no thought but this one, which floated to the surface of my mind like a slow bubble of air in a quiet pond: *Ah,* this thought said mildly, regretfully, *ah, the baby.*

I had given birth to Hedley three months before. She was upstairs in our lavender room, asleep in her lacy bassinet. My breasts were full of milk for her. *Ah, the baby.*

When the young woman disappeared like a rabbit into the hole at the back of the store, I turned my head to where the gunman stood. He was gone. Her scream must have shocked *him* as much as his gun shocked *her.* Truly it was a mighty scream. So he had fled. Evidently they had pushed each other away, just as the matching poles of a pair of magnets repel each other. Both were gone.

I walked to the rear of the store and then down into the basement where the clerk and her two colleagues were huddled—she weeping—the others looking pale and quite reasonably afraid. They certainly did not expect to see me.

I told them he had gone, suggested they call the police and then went calmly up to my apartment to see the sleeping baby. How would she look now to a mother who had just died?

I put it that way because surely that outcome was just as likely as the one that actually occurred. But at the time, the surge of fear the clerk experienced, which probably saved both our lives—and I do thank God for that—was not shared by me at all, not at all. There was no adrenaline rush, no speedup of my pulse, no cold sweat, just that single mild thought, *Ah, the baby.*

Now, you may think I was in shock or denial, or some trauma-induced, mercifully detached psychological state. But that wasn't it.

There was no aftershock—nothing that hit me days or weeks later with the realization, "Oh, my God, I almost died." No. I have read and thought a great deal about dying, and armed with good information—the information I have been sharing with you—I have no fear of death. You don't have to be frightened of it either.

FEAR IS THRILLING

And is fear always the enemy? Sometimes we deliberately play with fear just for the thrill of it, for the momentary exhilaration that it provides. Here are some examples: we climb into the roller coaster, screaming throughout the ride; we throw our bodies out of airplanes, yanking the rip cord on the parachute just in time; we go bungee jumping, whitewater rafting, rock climbing.

You can think of many more examples, I am sure, of times when we flirt deliberately with fear—when we take our life, so to speak, in our hands. What is the assumption that underlies all these choices? It is this: that we will survive!

If we didn't think we would survive, we wouldn't drop our bodies out of the plane. We wouldn't dangle off a rock face, we wouldn't run for the front car of the roller coaster, and we certainly wouldn't shoot through boiling rapids in a canvas kayak or a rubber raft. Right?

So what is the payoff when we willingly dance with fear? It's the intensification of our mundane lives, isn't it? It's the new pair of glasses through which our ordinary reality just doesn't look the same. And we relish that change, that expansion of the view, that moment of being lifted out of time. It's a thrill—as long as we know there's a way back.

Now—the fear of one's own death—the breath-stopping, throat-closing, heart-pounding fear that most of us taste when the doctor says, "You have a bad cancer" or "You have AIDS" or "You have three months"—that fear can also be experienced as a thrill. But only if you know—I mean *really* know—that you are in no danger. Death is perfectly safe, just as going to sleep is.

Imagine This

You are in the front car of the roller coaster. You slowly climb the steepest of hills. There is that pause at the top where you look down and see—with a nervous laugh—the vertical plunge you are about to take. It cannot be stopped. You grasp the bar. You scream. Is it terror or is it joy?

You know the roller coaster is 100 percent safe—you know that in three minutes the whole train will clatter into the shed and unload. You are along for the ride. Death is perfectly safe. And fear is just exhilaration and excitement filtered through dread.

How to Get Over Your Fear of Death

You will have to immerse yourself in the facts we have discussed together. You must really understand that you are different from your body and that you survive your body's demise. You are definitely *not* what you eat. To come to know this so thoroughly that you are no longer able to fear death will require some study and some daily practice.

If you have recently been diagnosed with a body-threatening illness, you are probably highly motivated and can master this material very quickly. Participants in Start the Conversation often get it in minutes—at the most, it takes six weeks. It depends on your own urgency and your willingness to suspend disbelief, to think and to read. Now let's tackle the matter of grief, and fear of grief as well.

ELIMINATING GRIEF

Once you understand what really happens when someone dies, you will certainly not experience grief. Remember the lion's roar—the jungle setting versus the zoo? Same stimulus—the sound of a lion right beside you—and two very different responses. OK, just like fear, grief is also unplugged when you *know* that the loved one has not been annihilated, done away with, extinguished, destroyed.

The hitch is that you have to know this *before,* not after, the death occurs. Otherwise, the shock of losing physical access to someone you love is enormous, especially if the loss was sudden and unanticipated. Once that shock has hit, it is virtually impossible to think clearly. New perspectives can't be assimilated well, if at all. Nor is it possible to deploy courage, that stiff-upper-lip approach so many men unfortunately try to use. We do such damage to our ability to feel anything at all if we try that approach for any length of time, though it does allow us to function as needed in the first few days.

As we think about losing the people we love, it is critical to notice the distinction between grief—a bottomless pit of sorrow that I dropped into over thirty years ago when my mother died—and sadness, which can be a sweet emotion, deepening and enriching us as it moves through our hearts.

If we do the necessary preparation to a sufficient extent, if we come to the solid conviction that all our dear ones will survive, then sadness, not grief, will become the context in which every death is experienced.

Here is one way to experience the difference between sadness and grief:

HEADING OUT OF TOWN

Assume that your beloved—your son or daughter, your husband, wife or lover, sister or brother, your very best friend—has been given a major promotion, which entails a transfer, a permanent transfer to Paris or Maui, or some other distant but wonderful spot many time zones away.

You and she have prepared for weeks—you have reminisced over all the wonderful times, you have resolved any unfinished business there may have been—and you have packed and loaded the car. Now you're on the way to the airport, your hearts are full—everything has already been said—you're silent and at peace.

Now her flight is called. At the gate you hug each other very tightly. There are tears. You will not be writing letters—you both know that. And after one or two attempts to call, you will each settle into a new way of life—a life that doesn't include each other. This is the way it will be.

In your car on the way home, you are full of feeling. There's a heaviness in your chest. For this is not a business-as-usual day. More than at any time in the years you spent together, you are aware of the depth of feeling you have for your friend.

She is so special, so dear. And your life together has been just wonderful. The unique individual she is now seems crystal clear to you—each facet of her complex personality sparkles in your mind's eye. Your heart is overflowing with a rich and exquisite blend of love and longing. You will miss her terribly.

But you will not go home and cry. Because you know your friend is on a plane headed to Europe or Hawaii. She has not been wiped out. She is alive and well. She is just unavailable at this time. Your somber mood in the subsequent hours, days or weeks is a passing temporary condition called melancholy or sadness. It is not grief. And there are interesting ways of working with and enjoying this normal, rich and utterly appropriate complex of feelings we call sadness. We'll make some suggestions in a bit.

JUST ONE THING MORE

Do you doubt that the intense pain of grief could be based *entirely* on the Annihilation Premise? You're right. There's another important component to grieving, of which I want to remind you now. It's that unpleasant business we covered right at the beginning, about the fine print on the contract, about the terms that govern our use of these bodies.

Particularly if the beloved's death is unanticipated, sudden, "premature," we hear this endless painful litany: "Why me, why this, why now?" We neglected to read the beloved's contract. So our anguish sounds like this: "Why my mother? Why my son? Why my husband, my very best friend? How on earth can this possibly be?"

I asked a fourteen-year-old actress whose mother had recently died of colon cancer whether her own heartbreak would have been eased in any way had she realized before the diagnosis that her mother would surely die one day, of something. She thought just a few seconds and then quietly said, "Yes, it would have made a tremendous difference to me."

REVISITING LILY

Back to our friends Lily and Frank. Theirs was such an interesting situation, because on the day of Frank's squash court heart attack and apparent death, he went to heaven, so to speak, and she went to hell. She sat beside her beloved and watched him die—in the middle of a sentence, abruptly, just when they both thought his crisis was over and they were safe. What a horror.

Frank's survival, his reassuring story of having been so blissful when he was "dead" and even his enduring lack of fear about the inevitability of dying again—these things haven't comforted Lily all that much. She remained, when I met her three years later, very much at the effect of the awful shocks she suffered that day.

Lily took a heavy double hit: first Frank's heart attack after the squash game, then the sweet interval in which he seemed OK and she could rejoice that he had made it through. And then, when her guard was down, the big one, his apparent death itself, with the clanging of alarm bells and the scurry of emergency personnel sweeping her out of the room. What could possibly make it worse? Maybe this: It was also her birthday.

The shock of what happened to Lily is still deep in her bones. It isn't that she doesn't believe Frank when he reminds her he was still himself. The Annihilation Premise has weakened its hold on Lily, at least intellectually. It's that she was caught completely unprepared, having believed, as most of us prefer to do, that death would visit them both decades later, when their grandchildren were grown and there was nothing for them to do but sleep—together.

Shock-Proofing Our Lives

It may still come about that way for Lily and Frank. I hope
for their happiness' sake that it does. But there is absolutely
no reason to believe that it *has* to be so. How then can we
shock-proof our relationships, all of them, so that when the
separations come, as they must, we don't come tumbling
down like a house of cards?

Shock Absorbers

Read your contract. Memorize its salient points. They are obvious: anytime, anyplace, everyone I love and myself. Death
must come. There is no other possibility. *And* there is no
death.

There is no death. This is the understanding that always
arises when the Premises of Annihilation and Associated
Concepts fall. To arrive at this conclusion, though, you have
to be able to think the evidence through calmly.

The Lion's Roar. Remembering that the neurological path-
ways are in place to transform your grief into another experience—sadness, let's call it—what should you do if you
can't quite believe, at this stage of our work together, that the
person you think you've lost is, for all practical purposes,
alive and well in another city?

Can We Really Master This? Absolutely. We have the natural tendencies of the mind on our side. For it turns out that
even addressing our minds *as if* we believed something to
be the case causes the mind to fall in step behind our would-
be conviction.

In other words, to acquire and strengthen the knowledge
that the beloved is being transferred out of town, not de-

stroyed, you will have to make an effort to train your mind. This is not hard either. It's the suffering we get stuck with if we don't train the mind that's really hard. So here's what to do.

ANNIE DOESN'T LIVE HERE ANYMORE

You're going to dialogue with your conventionally oriented mind *as if* you knew that the "relocation, not annihilation" concept we've been developing together is true. Assume you know that your friend Annie will be dying soon. This is the way that conversation between you (the Witness of your life) and your mind will sound:

Your mind punches you below the belt with one of these: "You are never going to see (talk to, hug, hear from, travel with, and so on) Annie again. You must feel just awful. What could be worse?"

You counter with this: "Listen, Annie is out of town. I won't be talking to her today, that's for sure. Just not today."

The mind comes back hard: "Yeah, but she's dead, you know. You won't be talking to her ever again. That's *never,* in case you're kidding yourself about this. As in not next week, next month or next year."

You reply, "Listen, as far as I'm concerned, Annie is not available today because she's out of town. I challenge you to show me what the difference is right here, right now, between Annie-out-of-town and Annie-you're-calling-dead. Confining your remarks to my experience *today and today only,* I want you to show me the big difference or any difference, for that matter, between Annie dead and Annie out of town."

The mind says, "Can I get back to you on that?"

Notice that you need to step back from your "I" in order to hear the mind's argument clearly enough to respond. You really *need* your Witness here. It's just fine to use "I" when you are countering the mind's assault because it's the real "I" who is speaking—the Witness of The Waking State Mind.

Your mind *will* get back to you on that, without a doubt. But not with some real difference between "dead" and "out of town." Because right *now*, there isn't any.

Let me share with you the experience that gave me my first real knowledge that this is so.

WHAT'S THE DIFFERENCE?

In 1977 I chose to go to an ashram in India—that's a monastery in the Hindu tradition—to immerse myself in meditation and an exploration of my relationship with God, whatever that was.

Let me hasten to add that I was also in an enormous amount of emotional pain, as I had been more or less since childhood. By no means had I fully recovered from my mother's death twelve years before. I was limping out of a flamboyantly failed marriage. And I was exhausted from solo parenting a most wonderful but challenging little boy. In other words, I was desperate. Let's say I was a highly motivated seeker. I had a burr the size of a boulder under my saddle.

My son went eagerly to live with his dad and stepmother, and I disposed of all my stuff—books, furniture, piano, plants, clothes, everything—gave up an exquisite apartment I had thought never to move out of and left for the other side of the world.

For the first nine months of my stay in Ganeshpuri, I grieved ceaselessly over my son. Yes, I had chosen to leave him, and yes, I knew there was no other choice. But still I cried over it every day and fell asleep each night longing for him. Whatever benefits I might later get from the discipline and holiness of ashram life, this longing to see Clement was the overriding focus of my mind. I was intensely grieving the loss of my son.

Then one night I had the following dream:

> *Clement, his dad and stepmother were entering their apartment building in New York. There was a light rain falling and his dad held a raincoat over his family's head to protect them. Noting this gesture and being aware that I was dreaming this, I thought,* That's touching and sweet; he really loves them. *Just behind that lurked a darker thought:* You can't protect anybody; he's kidding himself.
>
> *All three entered the elevator and Clement, noticing that the elevator ceiling had a large panel missing, as if someone needed access to the machinery on top, asked if he could ride up there. "Sure," his parents said (how flexible the rules are in a dream), and up he climbed.*
>
> *As the tenth floor approached, his stepmother called up, "Clement, do you have your key? We're home." Into the lengthening silence came a sickening sound, the sound of something rolling off the top of the elevator, hurtling down the adjacent shaft, landing with a muted thud ten floors below.*
>
> *Waves of horror rolled over me. I watched as his parents, refusing to believe what they had heard, called again up to Clement for the key. Then they realized that it was he who had fallen, painlessly, in his sleep (again that capricious logic of dreams), and was gone. Shock. And pain beyond bearing. My heart broke for them in that moment, for his dad especially, who loved that boy and wanted only to keep him safe.*

I awoke in that awful moment. My son had died. My heart was pounding, adrenaline racing through my body, which was drenched in sweat. The big ashram clock sounded the hour: *bong,* one.

My mind stayed immersed in the horror of that dream for a few seconds more. And then the waking state reality returned. Relief flooded over me. Clement was alive and well in New York City. His death had been a dream. Or had it? He was beyond my physical grasp. I could not hold him, hug him or see his sweet face. And the ashram had no phone, so I could not even hear his voice without traveling for hours into Bombay to make a call. The only photo I'd seen all year was of Clement dressed up for Halloween—as Dracula.

In what way did it help me, missing him as I had been, to know that he was alive? What was the big difference between knowing my boy was alive in this waking state and believing him to have died in the dream? Alive/dead, dead/alive, alive/dead, dead/alive—the two realities flickered back and forth faster and faster in my mind. Finally, they were one and the same. At that moment the clock sounded one. And Clement did indeed have the key.

Can this understanding endure the test of someone very dear going from well and strong to sick and dying in a short time? Here's an experience from the recent years of my life. See if you think it might work this way for you, too.

Michael Leaves Town

Michael was such a special guy. He had a way of being just the same wonderful guy with everybody—enthusiastic, friendly, focused on you fully when he was with you, turning you into the most interesting person in the whole world just for those few moments. And, oh, my, was he a handsome man—as in tall, dark and handsome, with an understated, rich and classy way of dressing; he looked like a model in a Ralph Lauren ad but without a hint of arrogance—he was just a natural, charming guy. Everybody loved Michael.

Michael showed up in my life at the perfect moment. I had been stretched to my limit running God's Love We Deliver and trying to be a reasonable mother to Hedley, who was three years old at the time. I was constantly exhausted, but even more painful, I was terribly lonely.

Not one of my old friends was in New York at the time. I was too tired and busy to make new friends, and though I was surrounded by wonderful people all day at work, I was sealed inside that bubble called "being the boss." Having to stay away from being personal with employees left me no one with whom I could just let down my guard and be myself—until Michael, who turned up as an eager volunteer chef one wonderful day.

He would breeze in on Thursdays to supervise a four-hour shift in the kitchen, and if I were around, which after a while I always was, he would sweep me into the privacy of the walk-in cooler for a hug, simultaneously cheering me up and preserving my dignity amidst the tubs of chopped onions and pots of fresh chicken stock.

"How are you, doll? You're looking gorgeous. (Indeed I made a fairly substantial effort in that direction on Thursdays.) You being good? (It was our joke—what the hell were my options not to be?) Got to get cooking. Catch you later." And he'd be gone.

Why those weekly hugs should have made such a difference for me, I'm sure I don't know. But they did, they really did. I was crazy about Michael and so grateful for his encouragement, even though I knew it was just the way Michael was with everybody.

We had a standing date on Wednesday mornings at 10:45. Michael would swing by my office in his lover the lawyer's maximum-strength black BMW and we would barrel up the West Side Highway (at way over the speed limit—with me driving) to Harlem to hear the ARC Gospel Choir. Oh, the joy of their music! How happy we always were to hear that choir.

This was the most delicious that life could be. It still seems so. And whenever I can, I still go up to Mt. Moriah Baptist Church to hear that choir.

It was Michael who insisted I start sharing my ideas about death with people who knew they were dying. I never felt ready to start teaching. Fear was the big problem—isn't it always? But Michael marched me down to the Manhattan Center for Living, where, though all the clients were dying, nobody uttered the "D" word, ever.

There was major New Age double-talk. Everybody was there to get "healed." Everybody was responsible for their own "healing," too. That way if you got sicker and died— and who did not—you had to add the insult of humiliation and failure to the injury of dying at twenty-five or thirty in the first place. *Argh!*

My take, as you know, has always been that no body gets out of here alive. Everyone else knows this, too. But denial was the anesthesia of choice at this center for living. And it always wore off at the worst possible moment, in the intensive care unit or the emergency room, when what was going on just could not be denied anymore.

That denial was keeping people from getting a handle on their fear or even confessing to one another that they were scared. What a sad and lonely, defeated death this nonsense yields.

But Michael was on the board at the center, so he booked us a room and a time slot, Tuesdays at 7:00 P.M., sat me down, held my hand and we began. Start the Conversation was born in 1989, with Michael as midwife and me laboring hard and clumsily to convey this unfamiliar, no-nonsense approach to death to a few young men and women with AIDS who were so very much afraid.

I share these details with you just by way of letting you know that Michael was the major—I'm tempted to say only—supporting actor in my show at that time. It's not that he was one of many encouraging friends; he was one of one. I still miss Michael.

As his AIDS progressed, Michael lost a whole lot of weight and began to stay home all the time. With the lost weight went his remaining strength, and Michael entered into what he called, with some sarcasm and disgust, his "granny phase." He was not amused. "This granny phase sucks," he would say in one of his weekly phone calls. But that was the extent of his complaint. He was not a whiner. Not at all.

"What's happening, doll?" Michael loved gossip and since he knew all the players in my daytime drama at the office, I could keep him entertained with tidbits I had saved up all the previous week. In so few minutes he would fatigue, not of my stories, which I always kept juicy, but of the effort it took him just to stay on the phone. "Love you, doll," he would say and then be gone.

Now Michael's apartment was an easy walk from mine and I really wanted to see him badly. But to my "Can I come over?" (New Yorkers absolutely never drop in), he would always say, "Not today, doll." And when I tried, "Is there anything I can pick up for you?" he didn't bite either. I was so frustrated by this that I finally said, "Is it just me, Michael, or are you not seeing *anyone*?"

That's when Michael said, "Look, you want to know what happens when somebody comes over here? They cry, I cry, we hug and we cry. Maybe we do this for twenty minutes. Then they go away. They feel better and I feel worse—much worse. What could be the point of that? If you love me . . . please don't come! If you love me, please don't come. I'll call you, but please don't come. I don't want you to see me like this. Please don't come."

The last time I saw Michael happened to be Valentine's Day, 1992—not that he went sentimental and granted me an audience, not Michael. No, there was a crisis at the office and I was terribly upset.

Since I was so shaken, Michael agreed to meet me for lunch at a restaurant near his place to prop me up. Mostly, his making that last lunch reflected extreme generosity. He knew how upset I was and he knew how little anyone other than he himself could have done to calm me down. "Only friend" is a big responsibility.

There were only three blocks to cover, but it took Michael forever to do it. I felt so ashamed of myself for letting him walk those blocks alone, as frail and vulnerable as he was. Later I reflected that he would not have wanted me to see him so weak and helpless in any case—that dignity, that pride.

If I tell you that the first thing Michael said after he dropped into his chair was, "Oh, Ganga, what kind of woman drags a guy *out* of bed on Valentine's Day?" perhaps you'll understand why I cherished him so.

He made me laugh. That was the comfort Michael brought. "Not a pretty picture," he liked to say.

So that was the last time I saw Michael in person in what was left of his flesh. He phoned one or two more times. He was fading so fast. But it was always "Hi, doll" and that the granny phase totally sucked. And if I really loved him, not to come by.

There was a phone call from one of Michael's sisters, who

wanted to assure me that the doctor was very optimistic about a new medication he was trying against Michael's latest mystery fever. Brian, Michael's doctor, expected the new drug to kick in any day. But Michael was in the hospital meanwhile.

"Not to rain on your parade," I said as gently as I could, "but when's your mom due back in town?"

"Not for two more weeks," the sister said. "Why, are you trying to tell me Michael might be dying?"

"What does the doctor say?" I ducked.

"He says this new drug might turn things around. He says we'll know in two or three days. He says Michael's very strong."

Brian can't stand losing Michael either, I thought. To the sister I said, "Why take a chance? How would your mom feel if she didn't get here in time? I think you should give her a call. Would she want to see him or not?"

I had upset the sister mightily and she was about to upset her mother even more. It was none of my business either, but it was the only way I had of thanking Michael for struggling out to comfort me on Valentine's Day.

I owed him and I owed the woman who had given him both his birth and his inevitable death. I had to hope that under similar circumstances, with my own son in a hospital bed far away, that someone would take on the hard job of calling me, the universal mother's prayer.

I didn't think Michael should die later rather than sooner, as his family, his doctor and his lover all did. That lanky, elegant body was all used up. Michael wasn't having any fun anymore and it was certainly time to move out. Knowing that he would still be exactly who he always had been, but free of the body's problems, I was praying for a sweet and painless moving day.

Everyone else was in awful anguish, of course. And there's

no question that it is much harder to let go of a son, a brother and a lover than a relatively new best friend. Nonetheless, though this last week of Michael's life was not a business-as-usual week, I did note that what was going on for me was sadness, not grief. I was aware of Michael steadily, but there were no tears. We had had such a wonderful time.

Knowing he was at Beth Israel, I went by early Tuesday evening just to be there for a little while. I knew I wouldn't see him because that was his wish. I thought just to stand outside his room, keep my vigil for half an hour, then go.

That's not quite the way it turned out. No sooner was I stationed in the corridor outside Michael's door than his lover came literally sprinting down the hall at me. "You can't go in there! You can't go in there!"

A wave of sorrow rose up inside me and flooded my heart. Tears came now for the first time. I felt such frustration at not being able to see my friend and deep humiliation at being spoken to in such a disrespectful way. I also understood the lover's duress. He hadn't intended to sound so cold and mean.

Michael's mother paced back and forth outside the room, stone-faced, way beyond tears. I pressed my back hard against the wall and struggled not to bolt and run. Michael's doctor, whose love for him was as major as mine, came and led me into a little consulting room, where he very sweetly and generously told me in detail what he thought was going on medically with Michael. I stared at Brian as he assured me that Michael's organs were "basically sound, and if we can just get this little infection in his brain under control..." Reading my expression correctly, he said, "You think I'm in denial, don't you?"

What could I say? We both knew what was happening, but Brian had fought so hard for every single day of

Michael's last six months and not just out of duty—out of love. Who wants to lose somebody like Michael?

I thanked him for taking the time to talk with me, which he certainly didn't have to do. And then I left. I was bursting with tears. I drove down to Friends In Deed, where the big Tuesday night support group, Cy's group, was in session. I sat down way at the back and just cried.

Whatever the tears were, they came and went like a summer thunderstorm, intense, powerful and fast. I went home and slept well, really well. Just at dawn came this dream:

> *Michael was stopping by to see me on his way out of town. He wore his nice Ralph Lauren blazer, his Hermès raincoat hooked over one thumb. He was casual, relaxed, elegant. But it was no big deal. It was a luxuriously unhurried encounter. We had, for the first time really, all the time in the world. No melodrama. Just a wordless deep love. It was good-bye for now. And there was nothing to say. I was aware that I was dreaming and I knew that Michael had died.*
>
> *But there was no problem at all about that. The problem had been not getting to say good-bye. So Michael had come over, as if on his way to the airport, to give me what I had missed and give it so fully that by the time we were through, I was absolutely content, at peace.*
>
> *At the very last, Michael drew his lover into the misty space we stood in and placed his hand in mine. "You take care of him for me now," was all he said. Then Michael's face grew chalky and his lover's grew clearer, more defined. I moved away from the dream, very still inside, very satisfied.*

I was still immersed in that sweetness about half an hour later when the phone rang. It was his lover to say that Michael had died last night, about eleven on April Fool's Day—our little joke. Because in fact Michael hadn't died. He had simply slipped out of town—in style.

I still see Michael's smile and feel his encouraging love. But I have never grieved over Michael. He's out of town at the moment, but one day he'll collect me at the airport in some fabulous car.

BEFORE, DURING OR AFTER

Now, you are no doubt saying to yourself, "Yes, I suppose it might work that way for you, but this seems more theoretical than real to me. Grief is normal, isn't it? Anyone who loses a child, for example, will certainly plunge into grief. How could it be any other way?"

On the contrary, this shift in understanding really does change the way a loss through death is experienced. This is what we've seen in over six years of offering this method of grief management to people who are themselves confronting such powerful emotional pain.

As I've already said, it makes a big difference whether the griever learns this perspective before, during or after the loss. Here are examples of all three circumstances, beginning with a woman who had already lost her son *before* she came to class.

PETER AND JOAN

Joan was a feisty woman in her mid-sixties who showed up about three years ago at an ongoing Conversation meeting, a meeting generally open only to people who have taken the six-week introductory class. She was smartly dressed as a tomboy grandma and had the forceful personality that went with her style. Joan's son Peter had died three months before, and she was both shocked and actively in grief.

We strongly suggested—insisted, in fact—that she enroll in Start the Conversation. In our experience, it's very difficult and often painful for a mourner to be dropped into a group in which the assumptions about death—that it's not final, not tragic and not at all the disaster it seems to be—are so very different from those that are the norm in our world.

But Joan was adamant. She couldn't and wouldn't wait for the introductory class. And she had tried the conventional grief groups—they just made her feel worse, not better—all those people feeling sorry for themselves, as she put it, and carrying on. Joan was fiercely determined to try another approach. Determined to relieve her extreme pain by whatever means there were, she wasn't going to budge.

She promised not to get angry if we didn't commiserate with her. Everyone in the group had either recently lost someone very dear or were themselves dealing with cancer or AIDS. Joan said she would do her best to understand.

So we let her stay. Naturally most of the first evening she spent with us was devoted to Joan. And in abbreviated form here's how it went.

Impermanence

JOAN: I never expected to lose Peter. We knew he was HIV positive, but we didn't think he had AIDS yet. We never imagined he would die.

GROUP: One or the other of you must surely die—that's true of every single relationship—not just yours with Peter. **Read your contract.**

JOAN: But I was supposed to go before him. Mothers are not supposed to bury their sons. **Where do you read that?**

GROUP: Throughout history, mothers have always buried their sons—and their daughters. In most of the developing world, women have to produce five or six children just to watch one grow up. **Get the bigger picture.**

JOAN: But I miss him so much. (Here the tears were streaming down her cheeks.) **But this separation was inevitable. 'Til death us do part, every one of us. No other possible outcome.**

GROUP: You can experience the feelings of missing him as the measure of your love for him. How deep do those feelings go? How much love is there? **The nature of love always includes longing.**

JOAN: (more tears) We were so close always!

GROUP: Not many people know a love like that. You and Peter were very blessed to have had so much joy in each other's company and to have lived in the same city. Did he ever go off on a long trip or live out of town?

JOAN: Yes, he went down the Amazon River one summer. I was frantically worried about him.

GROUP: So, what happened to your love? Did it go away when he did?

JOAN: (indignantly) Of course not! How could you think that?

GROUP: We didn't think that—that's just the point. The love is always there even when Peter's not—the love is what the relationship is made of—not the mere proximity. And how has your love for Peter changed since he died?

JOAN: It's stronger is the way it's changed. I think about him all the time. **The love itself does not require proximity.**

GROUP: Our point precisely. How much of each day is he in your thoughts? A whole lot. Well, what if instead of being dead, Peter were rafting down the Amazon right now? How would what you're going through be different? **Grief is based on the Annihilation Premise.**

JOAN: It would be completely different! At least I would know that he's alive somewhere! **He has not been annihilated.**

GROUP: He *is* alive somewhere. (And here we presented the proofs of survival that we set forth in Chapters Four, Five and Six.)

JOAN: So if what you say is true, I'm just beating a dead horse!

At this the group dissolved in laughter—and so did Joan—though the tears of sadness—her love and longing for Peter—were still streaming down her cheeks.

We had been working with Joan for under an hour—and she had gone from being submerged in grief to finding, despite her sorrow, a way to laugh at herself and at her obsession with Peter.

Let me give you a follow-up on Joan. Her grief over Peter was no minor matter. It certainly did not disappear in just one class. In fact, she has traces of it still, though, for the most part, it is sadness and a deep regret over Peter's death that Joan deals with now.

Joan has been coming to Start the Conversation steadily

over the years since we first met. She's always right in the front row, usually with her best friend Gloria, who propped her up through the worst of her grief. Gloria's a solid pal.

Gradually, Joan has become able to talk about Peter without the tears that flowed every single time during that first year. And I mention this just to emphasize that there's nothing in our approach to grief that stifles the natural flow of those tears.

This is not about suppression, nor is it about trying to force the mind into an artificial and untenable stance. You can't force the mind to do anything; you have to get its cooperation. You have to pull it toward you, so this is what we do.

Joan's grief was so intense for the first year that she really couldn't read any of the suggested books or use her mind constructively to build her understanding that Peter was alive and, at the moment, out of town, unable to come to the phone. She kept up one refrain, without interruption: "Why didn't I know about this *before* Peter died?"

Joan has a strong sense that this approach to loss would have shielded her powerfully from what she went through over Peter. We can't know for sure, in her case. That's why I want to tell you next about Connie.

CONNIE'S STORY

At the first meeting of Start the Conversation, I ask everyone to say just a little about what brought him or her into the room at this time. And usually, as you would imagine, people are there because someone they love is dying soon or has just died. Often there are health-care professionals, nurses especially, and then there are increasingly people who are themselves preparing to leave their bodies behind.

The common themes, no matter what the external circumstances, are fear and grief, which are always, on the first night of class, as thick and visible as fog in the room.

Connie is a sensible-looking middle-aged woman, neat and alert. When her turn came, she said something that no one had said before.

"I have three grown kids," said Connie. "And you know how kids are. They're healthy, thank God (so many of the mothers in the room are there because their kids are dying), but I realized not long ago that any one of them could die at any time. They could. Why not? And then I'm afraid I would lose my mind. So that's why I'm here. I don't want to go crazy if one of them dies."

Now this is a woman after my own heart. She had read the fine print. She had understood that in giving birth she had given death as well—given it to her children just as her mother had given it to her. Any time at all. Bright lady.

So she had decided to face it down before the fact instead of trying to figure it out afterward, half-crazy with grief. Brave lady. Sound move.

I made a point of calling attention to Connie's purpose. The same fear—that losing the child would mean losing my mind—had clobbered me when I gave birth to my son twenty-four years ago. I'll never forget that chilling moment when I realized how vulnerable he was, and myself as well, through him.

Because of my attachment to that newborn baby, because of that fierce love, the stakes in my life had gone way, way up. And even though the fear went underground almost immediately, I realize that it had muted my joy in the baby for quite some time.

Well, Connie made every class. And I gathered from her enthusiasm and her excellent questions that she was getting what she came for.

I was out of town for four days right after the course ended, and when I got home, there was a phone call from Cynthia O'Neal, who runs Friends In Deed, where I teach.

"Ganga," she said, "do you know which of the people in your last group was Connie?"

"Sure," I said, "she's the one who noticed that her kids could die. She's trying to get a handle on it ahead of time. Smart cookie. Why do you ask?"

"Because that's just what happened," Cy replied. "Two days after the course was over, her son died in a car crash on the West Side Highway at 103rd. There were five kids in the car; three were killed instantly, including Connie's son. So they called here to tell us what had happened and to have you give her a call. You were away, so I called to see how she was.

"And Ganga—she was incredible—I mean she was crying, but she was fine! She told me to let you know that she was fine. You might want to give her a call. I've never seen anything like this before."

I called Connie. It was five days after her son's death. Here's how our conversation went:

G: Connie, it's Ganga—how are you holding up?

C: You know, I'm fine, Ganga. I miss him. I miss him so much. But I know that he's all right. I'm sure I'll see him when it's my time. I'm not worried about that. It's just that I miss him so much.

I could hear the tears in Connie's voice, and I was relieved at that. She was not in denial; she was not in shock. Her sorrow was completely appropriate and normal. It would abate, in time. It wasn't that she would be fine later. She was fine right now.

Connie came to the next program I gave, some weeks later, bringing her best friend along. That's when I asked her if she had moments, in that first week after her boy's death, when she lost touch with her understanding of where he was.

She said that there had been several such moments, especially in the first few days. What saved her, she said, from sliding into despair, were the reminders her adult daughter, who lives with her, was able to provide. It seems that Connie had gone home after each class and shared with her daughter what she had learned. They discussed the ideas all week long, and together read the recommended books. So that, she said, is how come she did fine. And by the way, Connie said, her daughter was doing fine, too.

Connie had an unusual degree of urgency going for her when she started the course. She knew very well that one of her children could easily die and she knew she would have been crushed had that happened. She worked hard to acquire the conviction she needed. Note that even though Connie's son died just two days *after* she had completed her preparatory work, the brand-new framework she had built to contain her loss held fast. Comparing her experience of loss to Joan's, we can easily see that an ounce of prevention is worth, not just a pound, but a ton of cure. To really prevent debilitating grief from taking hold, the knowledge needs to be in place before, not after, the fact.

WE'LL TRY ANYTHING

Mona and Fred are a couple whose only child, their thirty-five-year old son, was in his last six months of life when they came to class. He had been a practicing attorney, though he was now too ill to work, and they were—Mona particularly—heartbroken in the extreme by his illness and impending death.

Mona and Fred are a reserved and dignified couple, very private people. It was easy to see how uncomfortable they were with the prospect of opening their sorrow to the scrutiny of strangers, myself as well as the others in the class. But Friends In Deed is one of the few places in New York where they wouldn't be the only ones going through this particular nightmare. And the warmth of that fellowship is a great comfort.

They were having what is known as anticipatory grief when I first met them. Mona's handsome face seemed unlikely ever to lift into a smile again and Fred had the weary resignation of someone who has been asked to deal with something that is just too much.

I can really understand why even old friends will sometimes dodge and abandon people who are in this sad state. The reminder of our own inevitable losses, the fear of not saying the right thing, of somehow making matters worse, and the guilt at being glad that it is happening to someone else, not ourselves, all conspire to isolate people just when they need the comfort of their friends the most.

So there, in their vulnerability and in their pain—and in the front row—were the toughest possible folks to turn around. I was very concerned that they would misconstrue my awfully no-nonsense approach and hear it as a lack of sympathy for their plight. Thank goodness, that didn't happen. I think they had been warned.

At any rate, on the very first night, I had to be quite merciless with Mona. She voiced the "Mothers aren't supposed to bury their sons" idea and extended it by saying that she shouldn't have to go through something like this.

"Wait a minute, wait a minute, Mona. Let me get this

straight. You expected to die first and that way your son would get to deal with the suffering you're having now? Very loving, Mom. I need to make a note of this. This must be love, huh?"

Mona got it on the spot. Mothers want to spare their children anything they can. That's just the way it is. She could see that in carrying the awful weight of this one, she was bearing a sorrow that he had been spared. She was able to find real comfort in that.

The class progressed through all six sessions. Fred and Mona made every one. In the course evaluation that each participant completes on the last night, Fred said that he had come truly to believe that his son's life would go on, even after the body was gone, despite the fact that such an idea was entirely foreign to him before he took the course.

And Mona said that she had come to understand how her son's impending death had not only hard lessons for her, but also some substantial benefits as well. And they both would have given anything, of course, not to lose their son.

As an update on their story, I met a woman last summer who had been at the funeral of Fred and Mona's son. I hadn't heard from them after he died, though I knew that had happened. "How did they do?" I asked her. I was so eager to know. Their friend said they were fine, absolutely fine. They were grateful for their child's life and they were confident that they would encounter him somewhere, sometime.

Now those are just three out of the hundreds and hundreds of comparable experiences that graduates of Start the Conversation have had. I chose them to illustrate the typical before, during and after results so that you can have reasonable expectations in your own work. Just remember that even if you have recently lost a loved one and are immersed in grief, it is still very helpful to work with this approach. It is unlikely that the person you just lost will be the very last one. You're going to have plenty of opportunity to make use of these tools, don't worry.

You really can unseat the grief. Is that worth working for?

NEW UNDERSTANDING NEEDS NEW LANGUAGE

In this section, we will take a closer look at that moment of separation—the transition we call death. It's important here to remember that when we die, we relocate, we leave, we move out, we go right on. We are not snuffed out, done in or done away with. We do not lose our life. No one can take our life; we can't even give it away or ditch it if we want to. We may in a moment of heroism believe that we have offered our life, but in fact what we have offered is our body. That's a big gift, to be certain, equivalent in magnitude to giving away your apartment and your car. Such an act would leave you homeless, to be sure, and without a way to get around—but it would not destroy you, because in fact, *nothing* can. *You* cannot be destroyed.

The word *annihilation* derives from Latin. At its center is *nihil*, which means "nothing," and up front is the prefix *a*, which comes from the preposition *ad*, meaning "to" or "toward." So annihilation indicates a movement toward nothingness, which is what most people think happens when someone dies.

Since words are the building blocks of thought and since what we are after here is to shift the way we think and therefore the way we feel about death, we need to look closely at the words and phrases we have usually used to describe it. And we need to come up with some more appropriate ones.

Here's an exercise: Use the space that follows to add all the words that you can think of to each of these short start-up lists. Don't avoid slang terms either, or worry about being in bad taste. Nothing could be in worse taste than misstating the matter when someone dies.

Nouns and Pronouns	Verbs	Adjectives	Expressions
deceased	died	mortal	fate worse than death
corpse	croaked	tragic	got what was coming to him
body	expired	untimely	dropped dead
the remains	deceased	horrible	met his maker
he	terminated	early	bought it
she	kicked the bucket	mangled	wiped out
I	destroyed	terminal	bit the dust

Notice how many of these words equate death with annihilation: *destroyed, expired, terminated,* and so on.

Can you create a second list of words that carries no implication of finality at all? Here's a list for you to add to:

took off	left the body
left	got promoted
went on	graduated
went to his reward	left town
met her maker	

You may think this exercise a mere matter of trying to find euphemisms—less scary words—for death. That is not at all the case. Human beings do not expire like so many library cards or driver's licenses—we go on interminably.

We have in common with matter itself the property of

being unable either to be created or destroyed. That's what is true for matter, the stuff of which the body is made. It is also true for us. We matter, after all, so much more than matter.

CONSIDERING SUICIDE

The most important thing to know about suicide is that it can't be done. What do I mean? Suicide is killing one's self. And killing one's self is just not possible. That's why all suicide, whether "successful" or not, is "attempted" suicide—that's all.

What is killed in a successful suicide? Only the body. That's the good news and the bad. Because if the reasons for contemplating suicide have to do only with physical problems—intractable pain, for an obvious example—then there is logic in considering suicide, since, as Benjamin Franklin put it, "He who quits the body quits at once all pains and possibilities of pains which it was liable to, or capable of making him suffer."

However, there are so many people thinking about suicide whose despair is not the result of being at a physcial dead end in the body. Depression, feelings of hopelessness, loss of a dear one, boredom, lack of direction, lack of love—these are some of the commonest reasons people suffer enough to want out.

It's important to note that wanting out, wanting to be free of pain, is a self-loving, not a self-hating, impulse. But the problem with wanting out via suicide is that *you* are still right there even though your body is not. Your dilemma is right there, too. But now there is no way to work it through. And work it through we must, for our lives' dilemmas are not mere accident, but the very puzzles that we set ourselves to solve.

WHAT IS SUICIDE

Think of it this way: You've been living in an apartment since childhood—a lovely apartment, in which you've been comfortable and very much at home. Decades have passed, though, and inevitably things have changed. The walls have some cracks that are quite beyond repair. There's dangerous stuff in the water because of the old-fashioned lead pipes. And the wiring is inadequate to take even a modest air conditioner, much less your new computer. Moreover, garbage has been piling up in the halls because the service elevator is always down, and the super has long since quit.

Now the owner of the building has figured out that it would cost more to fix the place up than he could ever make back, so he stopped paying his taxes on it last year and walked away. The city finally took title to the place, but not before the process of decay had accelerated a lot. The pipes have been stripped and sold as scrap—the electrical wiring, too.

You're still hanging in there, though, hoping against all odds that the neighborhood will somehow come back and with it this wonderful old building that has always been your home.

Finally the city cinder blocks up the windows and the front door is next. Endgame. You've been living in cold dark rooms without water in what is still your old home. But it just can't be your home anymore because it won't physically afford you a decent quality of life—not that you don't still love the old place.

So you finally make the necessary arrangements and move out.

Suicide.

All the inconveniences—all the impossibilities—of the old place are finished and forgotten. And you are still exactly who you always were, which, as we said earlier, is both the good news and the bad.

A Little Fable. Once in the Pacific Northwest a powerful bald eagle plucked a succulent salmon out of the river. Oh, it was a magnificent fish, and the eagle could hardly wait to get it back to her nest. A flock of crows, persistent bold scavengers, saw the salmon in the eagle's grasp and immediately took off after the fish. No matter which way the eagle flew, she couldn't shake the noisy tenacious crows and she couldn't get that salmon back to her nest.

Finally, in exasperation, the eagle relinquished her prize, which by then had some fairly substantial chunks pecked out of it. It was, in fact, the fish, that is, a very sorry version of its original plump perfection. Therefore the eagle could drop it without too much difficulty and make her solitary way home.

The crows, of course, had no further interest in the eagle and plunged directly after the flopping fish, making short work of it with relish when it hit the ground.

Now the eagle was a creature of some analytical gifts and with these she considered her recent experience with the fish. Her thoughts ran along this way: *There wasn't that much left of that fish by the time I gave it up. If it were the same fat fish I plucked out of the river, it might have been worth fighting for further. It had certainly passed the point of diminishing returns, and besides, it's not the last available fish, not by a long shot. Moreover, I have to notice that all my problems with those nasty crows disappeared when I dropped that fish.*

Suicide

We can choose to give up the body because it is useless to us in its present condition, it will never improve and all our difficulties—our ONLY difficulties—come from hanging onto it. Got that? But there's something not quite so straightforward—something more.

Suicide Class. We offered a class on suicide some months ago. It drew an interesting though small group of participants. There were six healthy-looking young gay men, all of whom told me they were HIV positive and exploring whether suicide would be a viable option for them later, when the disease made life in the body too unpleasant.

I asked Jose, who was sitting right in the front row, what he had determined was the purpose of his life and whether it had been fulfilled yet. "The what?" he said, drawing a big blank. "You know," I elaborated a tad, "the reason you're here, what you set out to do, your life's goals, your mission . . . is it accomplished or not?"

He had never heard any such question in his life and it stopped him cold. I suggested that before considering getting out, he might want to figure out what his business here had been and see whether he had made at least a dent in it—or not.

I went on building my usual case that the body is what we use to get around—like a car—or where we live—like an apartment—not what we are. Jose and his friends were following right along, clearly reassessing their situation in view of this new perspective.

Then in rolled Tony in his heavy-duty chair. "Sorry to be late," he said, "but I've got three buses between here and

Brooklyn and some of them can't pick up the chair, so I have to wait."

"So look," said Tony, "here's the deal. I'm twenty-four and I've been in this chair all my life. I'm not getting out either. I've got muscular dystrophy and this is the best it's ever going to be. So what's the point? My mother says it's her business if I kill myself, but I don't see how anyone can have anything to say about this but me. She doesn't have to live in this chair."

I glanced at Jose and his buddies to see how they were hearing Tony. They were very quiet.

"OK, Tony," I said, "you're making some sense to me. But let me ask you this. What was the purpose of your life and when did you complete it, which I assume you must have done, or you wouldn't be packed and ready to check out?"

"Purpose of my life—purpose of my life?" Tony almost shrieked out the words. "I've been working on that for the past fifteen years. It drives me crazy. I haven't got a clue. There's got to be some point—I just can't see it. I think about it all the time."

"That's pretty interesting, Tony," I said. "I asked Jose that same question just before you got here and he didn't have a clue either, but not just about the answer. He had never heard the question before. So it looks like you got at least a fifteen-year head start on these guys, who were probably playing football and getting laid while you sat in that chair. Congratulations. Looks to me like you're way ahead of the game."

At that moment another wheelchair rolled into the room and in it sat Carmello Gonzalez, a few years older than Tony but under thirty still, and with so profound a case of cerebral palsy that as he began to speak, I panicked. At first I couldn't understand a word—not a single word!

Carmello's body seemed put together all wrong—things were on sideways that were supposed to be straight up and down—crucial things, like his head and his hands. And inside that prison of a twisted body was a crackerjack brain and a stand-up (except that he had to sit down) comedian with an endless store of material. Tony turned out to be his straight man—they were daily telephone buddies and had been wisecracking together at the walk-around world for years.

They were very, very funny—and the object of their humor was people like ourselves, who, confronted with one or two young guys in wheelchairs, go through some gyrations that are, to Carmello and Tony, predictable, familiar, wildly inappropriate, absurd and darkly funny. Together they were the verbal equivalent of Callahan, the quadriplegic cartoonist whose work is outrageous, tasteless from the perspective of the "normal" world and also very successful commercially.

I guess you've noticed, as I did with Tony and Carmello that evening, that the subject of suicide had disappeared. All I did was point out what was obvious to everyone in the room: These two young men had major gifts of intellect and heart to give. They were sparkling with wit, they were enjoying themselves mightily and we were enjoying them too. There was no way their lives were through, even though physically they didn't have much to look forward to, nor were there many choices they could make.

It's easy to undervalue the gifts of mind and spirit. So much importance has been accorded the body in Western culture.

Remember that movie *Whose Life Is It, Anyway?* The hero is an accomplished sculptor, a successful guy with a little red sports car and a ballet dancer as his lover—a perfect life, a life lived in and for the body—a basic American dream life.

And then he runs his little red sports car under a tractor trailer. By the time they patch him up, he can't move his body from the neck down. Now he's a quadriplegic and always will be. The doctors tell him he's lucky to be alive, but, you know what, he doesn't think so. Maybe you wouldn't either. Would you?

Our hero's perspective is that his life is of no value because he can't make love or make art anymore. And that's all he knows. So the plot turns around our hero arguing, successfully as it turns out, for the right to refuse dialysis, the treatment that has been sustaining his body.

The doctors, in this case, are the bad guys. They just don't understand his predicament is the hero's view, and if they were sitting where he is, they would choose as he has to duck out and be done with it. The ballet dancer lover supports his decision entirely—I'm guessing their conversations weren't all that lively. And he must have been one amazing lover for her to agree that she has no other comparably meaningful use for his company. Oh, my.

The movie ends with our hero in his hospital bed, victorious, waiting to die.

Now, I don't know how this strikes you. I remember at the time being quite disgusted with this outcome—and not for the reason you might think. Whose life is it anyway? It's his life, of course. But what kind of a life is it? That's the real question. Evidently it's a life whose only purpose was sculpting and screwing. Those being impossible, our hero has run clean out of ideas, out of steam. Would you?

Stephen Hawking, the great theoretical physicist, hasn't moved a muscle on his own for close to twenty years. He seems to have made some contributions, though. And Franklin D. Roosevelt ran the government from a wheelchair. So what are the possibilities in this life?

LAST VISIT WITH JOHN

John Roth, whom I've talked about quite a bit already, was nearing the end of his life in this body and was at home in bed in Brooklyn, waiting to die. I put it that way because there were no real options for John except to wait it out: he was blind and had been for about a year—he was too weak to walk around anymore and he had no unfinished business with anyone in his life, as he had been winding down and tidying up his relationships for several years.

I went out to see him on a clear Saturday afternoon in March because I was going to be out of town for several days and I knew that John would probably die while I was gone. He was especially dear to me as a student and as a human being, and I wanted, for my own sake as well as his, to see him once more before we went our separate ways.

John was dozing when I arrived, so I spent some time with Barry, his lover and companion of many years. Barry had been taking care of John and keeping up with his full-time teaching career for quite some time. Barry served his dying friend with real joy. There was not the undercurrent of resentment that is so usual in these circumstances. Barry was palpably weary, but he was doing well.

John's mother was expected in a few days, and our sense was that John would probably be on his way after that. Barry had planned his summer trip to Europe—he had friends in several cities who would welcome and care for him when John was gone. I was so pleased to see that he had planned to take good care of himself in this way.

John woke up after a bit. I went in and sat on the bed, and took his hand. There was an exquisite patchwork comforter smoothed over John. Buttons and bits of textured cloth were sewn at intervals on the comforter, so that wherever his hands moved, there were interesting and varied encounters for him to have. John's friends, of which he had many, had made the quilt for him with so much thoughtfulness, so much love.

"Your hand is cold," was the first thing John said. How frail he was. I withdrew my hand and let it rest on the quilt, where he could still feel that I was there.

John and I had talked about this moment off and on for years. Which of his medications ought he to discontinue, he had wondered, to leave easily when the right time came. It wasn't quite a conversation about suicide, but it was the closest we had come. And this was clearly that time.

So I asked him whether he had any thoughts about suicide now—blind and in a diaper in his bed. There was a pause before he answered me, and then, in a weak but unemotional voice he said, "I don't even understand why that question would arise."

We said nothing more and in a few minutes he was asleep again. But it was clear to me then, as it is today, that John was so loved and so comforted by that love that for him, despite the mess his body was in, the question of suicide was meaningless. He was all right as he was and as far as death was concerned, he could wait.

I saw John's obituary in the *New York Times* as I headed back from that weekend trip. He had waited to see his mom and then gone peacefully, very easily on his way.

CONSIDERING SUICIDE

Here's a list of questions to consider:

Are your problems physical or emotional/spiritual?

If they are purely physical, have you explored every possible means to relieve your physical pain?

Have you exhausted all means of bringing love and encouragement to someone else? Happiness, it's been observed, is a by-product of an effort to make someone else happy.

Have you accomplished what, in this life, you set out to do?

Are all the relationships in your life resolved in a way that leaves everyone free of any painful burdens created by you?

Are you free of debt?

Is your desire to get out of here something that your loved ones are aware of and can accept?

Who will suffer if you leave?

Who, beside yourself, will suffer if you stay?

Will the manner of your departure be so messy as to traumatize the people who find your vacated body?

ONE MORE SMALL STORY

My father was a heavy cigarette smoker all his life. I remember the packs of Lucky Strikes, then Camels, all through the 1940s and 50s. I remember the sound of his mucousy morning cough and the smell of those first few cigarettes that he woke up early to have.

He never managed to quit for more than a few days at a time, and then the emotional price was so high (he was meaner and more irritable than ever) that we were all relieved when he returned as he always did to the one thing that seemed to keep the lid on his terrible temper.

Emphysema had begun to shorten his breath by the time I left for college in the late 50s, and he switched to a filtered, mentholated brand so that he could go on smoking as many cigarettes as he was used to.

The handwriting was on the wall, though, and by the time my mother died in 1965, shortness of breath had slowed him way, way down. There isn't any help for emphysema; it can be slowed (of course by not smoking) but not reversed, and my dad continued, as so many of his generation did, to smoke until he had to choose between smoking and breathing.

That's when he tried suicide. He had gone to Arizona to see if there was an easier breath to be drawn in the dry clean air. There wasn't. I picked him up at the airport—we rolled a wheelchair onto the plane—and I drove him to his apartment, where his doctor (you can see that this was twenty-five years ago) examined him and heard his frustrated account of all that arduous travel and no relief.

I was in the adjoining room, unpacking the suitcase, and I heard my dad say, "Tell me, Doc, will I live to the graduation?"

My sister was graduating from medical school in one week's time, and this was the focus of his life, the achievement he needed to see.

"Yes," I heard his doctor tell him, "I don't see why not, but I'm giving you round-the-clock nurses, 'cause you can't take care of yourself anymore. This way you'll be able to stay home. Otherwise, we're talking about a nursing home."

He consented to the nurses in two twelve-hour shifts and made the graduation in a wheelchair. But he made it. Three days later, the night nurse came in half an hour early—the day nurse had already left—and hauled him in from the ledge of his living room window, fifteen stories off the ground.

He was furious at having been thwarted and gave her, as she described it, "one hell of a fight." There was a penciled note on a torn scrap of paper by his bedside: Dr. Elsa Stone and a telephone number, Ingrid Stone and my number, too. Nothing more.

In other words, he was willing to have his daughters, one of whom had just begun a rough internship at Yale University, come down to the hotel and try to identify what was left of his body in bloody pajamas when it hit the ground.

Not cool. It would have taken both of us years to recover from the sight of that. And because my dad had satisfied all the criteria I listed above and had no way to make use of his body, getting rid of it made all kinds of sense for him. But there had to have been a less devastating—a more "considerate," as we used to say—way to do it.

SUGGESTED MOVIES

Fearless—Jeff Bridges, Rosie Perez

Shadowlands—Anthony Hopkins, Debra Winger

CHAPTER NINE

HOW TO PREPARE: REGRET-PROOFING YOUR LIFE

A YOUNG WOMAN WHOM I knew quite well when she was a teenager showed up at one of my introductory classes. I hadn't seen Heidi in many years. She had just turned thirty, she told me, and was looking wonderful, too, with the silky blond hair and robust good health of a well-nourished, upper-middle-class kid.

She'd had such a bumpy adolescence—and I was relieved to see that she seemed to be in one piece. "We'll talk afterward," I said, as it was time to start. During the question-and-answer period Heidi raised her hand.

"I've just been diagnosed with AIDS," she said. "And all I can think now is that my clock is ticking so much faster than everybody else's. It's not fair."

"Your clock's not ticking any faster, Heidi," I said. "It's ticking much louder, that's all."

REGRET-PROOFING YOUR LIFE

If you were to live today as if you knew you would be dying tonight of a stroke, say, in your sleep, what (if anything) would you do differently? If the answer is "not much," then you've got the life you had in mind for yourself. Good for you! I mean that.

Most of us tell ourselves that we've got time to make the important changes that would bring our lives more closely in line with our goals. And maybe we actually do. But what if you got a call from your doctor today and learned that instead of decades to get it all in, you had just a few weeks or months. How depressed would you be?

I started considering this matter back in 1964 when it was clear that my mother, who was fifty-four years old at the time, wasn't going to get much older. That cast her rather detailed plans for retirement in a very different light. My mother hated her job. She complained about it all the time. She was a "people person" stuck working as a research librarian. She said it was dry, lonely and boring.

But people didn't change jobs much in those days. So she sustained herself with dreams of her retirement when she would travel, paint, write her book, be happy. That happiness was waiting for her . . . it was just eleven years away. But she died of Lou Gehrig's disease at fifty-five. Whoops.

I'll be fifty-five this year. And sitting at my desk, sharing the big lesson of my mother's life with you on a snowy winter day, I am doing exactly what I would choose to be doing on this, my very last day.

THINKING ABOUT TIME

Hedley and I were driving down to her school last year when she was in first grade. Concepts about time were still a little fuzzy for her. There was a party coming up at school, which she had been looking forward to for weeks. Finally, in the car that morning, I was able to tell her that the party was tomorrow. Here's how our conversation went:

H: Oh, great, the party is tomorrow, I can't wait. How soon is tomorrow?

G. As soon as today is finished, it'll be tomorrow.

H: So when the party starts, it'll be tomorrow?

G: Actually, when the party starts, it'll be today. It's never tomorrow, it's always today, right?

H: MOM!!!

As usual, I'm saying something very simple and obvious here. But notice this: All the parties we will ever attend or have ever attended took place in some today or other. Call up a few memories of past parties or important events in your life. Notice that you are enjoying (or wincing at) those memories right here and now. Today. That's it. That's all we've got.

Time is the *only* nonrenewable form of wealth. Money comes and goes—people have reversals of fortune all the time. Even health can be regained again and again, as long as we have these bodies.

But time, which we joke about "killing," "finding," "losing," "wasting," and "saving" is our *only* asset, really. I don't mean future time. We can plan for the future, worry about it or use credit cards to spend its money *only* in the present moment, right now.

And I don't mean past time either. We can try to forget about the past or we can try to remember it, whatever suits us. We can dig around in our memories for the treasures— for the lessons, for the significance of the past. But we can *only* do those excavations right here, right now. So *now* what?

Here we are together in this very moment. And it is the only one we have. We may get more moments in the future, but they'll be the present moment when they arrive. All the time in the world is just the time we are spending together right now, you know.

We've all heard the old saw "There's no time like the present." Turns out there's no time *but* the present. Yes, the past *was*. And yes, the future *will be*. But only the present moment *is*.

Your time is your life—meaning we can only live our lives in this particular moment, right? So what I call "regret-proofing" amounts to choosing to spend the moments you do have, which are limited to these very ones, in a manner that reflects your nature, that embodies your values, that brings you happiness or peace.

Since time is the only currency of any value—the only thing we can't replace—it behooves us at least to be aware of how it is spent. We would never let a twenty-dollar bill just fall to the floor. Why would we want to be any less protective of twenty minutes?

I'VE WASTED MY LIFE

A dignified-looking man in his late fifties recently came to one of my introductory lectures. He paced around restlessly at the back of the room, which happens from time to time. Listening to talk about death is no easy matter, especially for people who have recently been diagnosed.

This particular evening there were about forty people in the room. When I finished an overview of my approach to what I like to call "mortality concerns," I asked if there were any questions. The pacer, now halfway out the rear door, leaned into the room and punched out these words at top volume, red-faced, angry and full of despair: "I'm fifty-nine, I'm fifty-nine, I've wasted my life. Wasted my life. Now I've got AIDS, and what was the point of my life? I've wasted my time. Damn it. Damn it. What was the point?"

Now this breaks my heart. But I only had a few seconds before he bolted out the door, so there wasn't time to be gentle or sweet.

"Snap out of it," is what I said. "It's not over yet. So get a grip. Whatever you figure your life is about, get a handle on it now. Most people live a lot longer than you have without figuring out what they came here to do.

"What's your life about? How should I know? You may not have an answer to that one either. But you sure do have the question right. And you have some real urgency going for you. I'll bet you figure it out fast."

This man had woken up in his sixtieth year of life to the sound of his own ticking clock. In fact, the alarm had gone off. And he was wide awake. Now what?

What has changed for him? Both everything and nothing. Nothing, in fact, has changed except that he put on his glasses, checked out the fine print on his contract, noticed that his occupancy of the body was a moment-to-moment deal and freaked out.

And everything has changed because he recognized the need to make something of value of his life and saw that time to do so was all he cared about. He will not be wasting time, killing time, marking time or losing time—not now and not ever again.

BODY TIME

Let me frame these remarks a little differently before we move on. We all know the concept of the biological clock— that is, the limited period of fertility in a woman's life after which she can't use her body to make babies anymore. Now, some women who haven't had kids by the time their mid- to late thirties arrive can become very focused on setting up their lives so that they can have those babies.

They get urgent around the matter because they know there's a limit to the time in which they can have those babies. And having those babies is something they must do for their happiness and to live the life they had in mind. They would regret endlessly not having had those kids. This is an obvious example of knowing what's important to us and focusing our attention on doing what we must to get there from wherever we are.

In just the same way, the man at the back of the room knew there was something he wanted to do (though he wasn't quite sure what) that he hadn't done yet. And now, with the realization that his time was limited, *he* got some urgency too.

The biological clock, that is, the "body time," as one of my friends called it, is all we're talking about in both cases. And we all have that biological clock, of course, it's ticking away even as I write, even as you read. Can you hear yours?

You do remember that no body gets out of here alive, right? And you do know for sure that whatever you actually are, it's certainly not that thing you get around town in, right? Whatever we may be, as individuals, as human beings, it is not limited to the body—not at all. I hope we have made this point thoroughly by now.

Therefore the urgency of which I speak is not about *who* we are, but rather about what, if anything, we want to accomplish while we have these bodies, while we are here.

A friend of mine has the following message on her answering machine: "This is not an answering machine, it is a questioning machine. And the questions are: Who are you and what do you want?"

Neat. I like that so much. Here's the rest: "If you do not

know who you are and what you want, please call back when you do."

Who are you and what do you want? Without getting a handle on these two questions, there's no way to make the choices you would wish you had made if this were your very last day.

You Already Know

This is probably as good a time as any, don't you think? Why not grab a piece of paper now, while you're still aware that it's important, and jot down the ten or twelve qualities you like best in yourself and the five or six things you dreamed of doing when you were too young to know that you couldn't do it all.

You'll notice right away that the aspects of your own personality that you feel happiest with can be nurtured and emphasized anytime. You can *be* the human being you want to be immediately.

Clearly, whether you get to *do* it all or not depends on how well you use your only available time, yup, today. And then, of course, it depends on how many todays you wind up getting. That's why doing what means the most to you *first* makes great sense.

Of course, it helps to know what that *is*. Or, until you've discovered your own best reason for being here, you can at least avoid doing what you know is beside the point—no more killing time, but perhaps much more relaxing and enjoying the people and activities you love.

So the strategy is to choose to do today only what you would consciously plan to do on your last precious remaining day of life. Or, turn it around. If you wouldn't choose to do this on your last afternoon, why on earth would you consent to do it now? I call this strategy regret-proofing. Can you really afford to live some other way?

THE LAST PICTURE SHOW

I called my friend Stanley in St. Louis last year. Stanley is an amazing and prolific fiction writer. He's also funny as hell—on paper. His own situation isn't at all funny, though. In the thirty years since I studied Faulkner with Stanley—he's a brilliant professor, too—Stanley's been sitting with multiple sclerosis. And I do mean sitting, as in wheelchair or couch. Not funny for Stanley—not funny for anyone, truthfully.

But can he write! In the three decades I've known him, Stanley has published six or eight big outrageously funny books, all raved about by the critics, all more or less ignored by the reading public.

And meanwhile his physical condition deteriorates, slowly, slowly taking him toward his death—as have the last few breaths you took while reading this. Stanley's sixty-four. And he's terrified. Because Stanley knows for sure that when death comes, it'll be the end of him, not just his bulky deadweight body.

When we spoke some years ago about my course and I said I could make a solid case that we are not the body thing we get around in, Stanley was furious with me. "Don't lie to your customers, Ingrid!" he barked at me and changed the subject fast.

So this time I called to tell Stanley that I had met a fan of his—a man who owned a copy of every book and short story collection Stanley had ever published and who read passages to his wife constantly, the rare tears of laughter watering his cheeks. "How can I match his reactions?" said the wife, with a tender little shrug. Stanley's writing gave her husband such happiness. That was more than enough for her.

So I called to describe this maximum-strength fan to Stanley—this has got to be tonic to any writer—and especially to one in a wheelchair—also to see if I could get Stanley to drop his fan a note. And as the conversation wound down, Stanley said, "Joan and I are going to the new Woody Allen movie later this afternoon. Have you seen it?"

"Not going to see it either," I replied. "The guy's got the morals of a toad on a good day, and he's so self-absorbed as to be totally boring—to me, anyway. Besides . . . I would never choose to see a Woody Allen movie—any Woody Allen movie—on the last afternoon of my life, which as far as I know, could very well be this one."

"Jesus, Ingrid, you got something wrong?"

"Not as far as I know," I replied. "But I did read the fine print on my contract a couple of years ago and I noticed that *what* was going to happen was already down there. It was the when, where and how that were up in the air. It did mention anytime, anyplace and any old way, though.

"I figured out I'd be smart to make my choices with that in mind, and there's no way in hell I would spend even five minutes of my last afternoon at a Woody Allen—or any other—movie. It's just not my idea of a good enough time."

"Jesus, Ingrid, I'm sorry I asked." He was, too.

Now notice that I am not suggesting any simplistic formula for deciding what is a worthwhile activity on *your* last day. The only "should" I can attach to this suggestion is this one: It should be something that makes you happy, something that you really enjoy. Stanley is crazy about Woody Allen. That movie might indeed be his best choice.

As a follow-up note, Stanley died a few days after his

sixty-fifth birthday, still holding court and wisecracking with his friends, living Stanley's perfect life.

The fact is that your body is yours for a limited engagement only. Of course, you are not confined to or defined by that physical thing. Hold that thought. You can add, if you wish, the idea that, like an actor, you will go on to other roles when the long-running play you're currently starring in closes.

The truth about life on earth is tough to keep in view. You may notice that it makes everything seem terribly precarious. Perhaps this makes you tense and worried so that you can't fully enjoy your life anymore.

Listen, every physical thing IS that precarious. I hate to have to keep saying this. You could skip this part and just go back and read Chapter One. But really, there's no question of WHAT is going to happen (to you, your family, your friends, your career, your house, your dog). It's just a matter of when.

That being the case, the challenge becomes to develop a frame of mind that embraces this reality without generating a mountain of anxiety. Here's one approach.

Gratitude Is the Attitude. I happened to catch Joan Rivers being interviewed by Barbara Walters the other night. At one point, Barbara asked whether Joan would ever relax and assume that her career was secure. Joan replied that she never stopped pushing because she always knew that one day she could wake up and it would all be gone. And that's a scary proposition, is it not? Especially in view of the fact that death definitely will come, and it *will* one day all be gone.

That's why, Joan added, she always said, "Thank you, God," each time she went on camera. Then she hedged her bet and said, "Well, it can't hurt"—meaning, I gather, that even if no one were listening, a little thank-you goes a long way.

This is a very sound strategy, not just from a spiritual standpoint, but a purely practical one as well. Here's why: The mind cannot be both thanking and worrying at the same time. That thank-you is what overrides the fear. It feels wonderful, too.

So it turns out that "count your blessings" is the most practical advice we can either get or give. People with a routinely high level of anxiety, as Joan has and as I do, often figure this one out. It serves us really well.

Once again, it's about pulling the realization that everything is temporary toward us, not attempting to bury it or push it away. That's the way to sail up over the fear.

PATTY'S WAY

My good friend Patty moved to Los Angeles from New York a few years ago. We teased her about the possibility of death by smog or earthquake. Patty said that both were more to her taste than death by subway mugging or random shooting, which are some of the options available in her previous neighborhood. To each her own, we agreed, and off she went. She and her husband, a swell guy named Dennis, did well out there and bought a house in Sherman Oaks, where my daughter and I visited her a while back.

"Oh," said Hedley, as we turned into their flower-filled, lovely little street, "this is paradise, Mom. It's clean, it's warm, it's pretty, there's no chewing gum stuck on the sidewalk— LET'S MOVE HERE."

The house, propped up on stilts on a hillside, was spacious and pretty, too, with a big view of the San Fernando Valley and the mountains beyond. There was a pool, a patio, flowers everywhere. And Patty, newly escaped from the gritty Upper West Side of New York, where there's always chewing gum stuck on the sidewalk, was appreciating every single thing about her new home. She was amazed at her good fortune and grateful for every breath that she drew in this enchanted place.

"But Patty," I said, "there's no actual land under this house, dear. It's sitting on toothpicks over thin air! How much earthquake would you need to topple it into the valley. And how do you sleep?"

"You know, Ganga," she said, "I've thought a lot about all that—Dennis and I both have. We've decided just to enjoy it while we have it, day by day. That's all we can do." And as an afterthought she added, "We're so grateful to be here."

The earthquake that was centered in the San Fernando Valley and that leveled big pieces of Sherman Oaks left Patty's toothpick house standing—at least for now.

I tell you this story to make the point that there are indeed ways to stay in touch with the inherent impermanence of things and not have your happiness sabotaged by worry and fear. Enjoying it day by day, being so very grateful for whatever you may have—this *works*.

Can you imagine what life would be like if every event were experienced as if it were the very last chance at giving love or eating ice cream? How very fully present we would be.

A FAMILY IN LOVE

Twelve years ago I was doing hospice volunteer work here in New York City. Barbara Rice, the volunteer coordinator at Cabrini Hospice, called to see if I could spend four hours with a family on Park Avenue in the Nineties. The patient was a lawyer with a slow-moving but deadly brain tumor. His wife had been taking care of him at home for many months. She just needed a break, a night out with friends, dinner and the theater. I jumped at the chance.

Mrs. White introduced me to the kids—there were two

boys and a girl, all under fourteen. I guessed that the youngest was about seven. And they seemed quite cheerful and matter-of-fact, having settled in for the long haul with their dad. Mr. White was a solid, nice-looking man, sitting back against an array of pillows in a wide and comfortable-looking bed. He didn't look sick. But when his wife began to give me instructions and he didn't participate at all, I understood that the tumor had somehow affected his ability to speak and think. But not, evidently, to feel.

His younger boy charged into the bedroom as we stood there talking. He bounced up onto his dad's bed, hugged him hard, saying nothing much, and then bounded out of the room. Mr. White's face, previously without expression, reflected such a pure uncomplicated joy. It was breathtaking to see—no self-consciousness, nothing held back, simple full feeling without embarrassment or shame.

Mrs. White went on with my instructions. The pizza had been ordered for supper—he and the kids would share it on the big bed. For dessert he could have Häagen-Dazs coffee ice cream, which he really loved. I was to feed it to him and should be careful not to give him too much. A few spoons would do. I told her we'd be fine and she left.

The pizza was over with and the kids in their rooms when I went to get the ice cream. I let it soften up for a few minutes, then set the whole pint on a plate and went in to see Mr. White. I pulled a chair over to the bed, tucked a napkin in under his chin and gave him the first spoonful. He opened his mouth dutifully, like a child, and then closed it expertly over the smooth little mound of ice cream and the heavy silver spoon. Then "Ah . . . ," he said. "Ahh." And in no particular hurry, he opened his mouth again.

The second spoonful went in exactly as the first had. "Ah . . . ," he said. "Ah . . ." His pleasure in the ice cream was so simple and touching. He was guileless as a very young child, so engrossed in what was going on in his mouth. I offered the third spoonful—the fourth, the fifth. "Ah . . . ," Mr. White said after each one. "Ah . . ." And the jaw would drop again, ready to receive the next bite. "Ah . . . ah . . ."

We had a rhythm going. We were in a slow dance together. Nowhere to be but here, with the ice cream and the spoon. "Ah . . . ah . . ." Finally it was all gone. I hadn't had any reason to stop as long as there was anything left. I knew he wasn't going to report me to his wife. What kept me spooning ice cream was that he received every single mouthful as if it were the very first. There was no "fade" for Mr. White. He was always tasting the best coffee ice cream for the very first time. What great good fortune.

I have mulled over the many lessons of my evening with the White family. And I think that the most important thing I learned was that because everyone knew that Mr. White would not be around indefinitely, people expressed their love for him whenever the impulse showed up. They didn't assume that a hug was inconsequential or could just as easily wait. They were aware that his presence was precious. So without any words and in a perfectly natural way, they let him know.

And I will never forget Mr. White, the emperor of ice cream.

SUGGESTED MOVIES

This Is My Life—Julie Kavner
Charlotte's Web—Hanna-Barbera animated film

CHAPTER TEN

DEALING WITH DYING

W E ARE BACK WHERE we began. Someone you love is dying—dying now, dying soon—someone you love very, very much. And you are in terrible pain.

Thirty years have passed since my mom died. The pain of those days has long since faded. But the memory of extreme pain, like the pain of a bad burn, is vivid. So I understand what you are struggling with right now. That's why I wrote this book. It's for you.

YOUR OWN PRIVATE EARTHQUAKE

How much devastation this shocking event will cause depends on several factors, not many of which are in your control. How close to the epicenter of your heart does the dying person live? Literally? Has your beloved been living *with* you, so that the structure of your everyday life will be radically changed?

Did you quake-proof the structure beforehand? Did you discuss, in other words, the inevitability of this parting of the ways? Or has this tremor woken you in the middle of a dream, a dream of going on together forever or at least into the foreseeable future (as if the future could be foreseen)?

This is the moment to reach for the tools you have been acquiring and **use** them.

Tool: *Your Beloved Is Not Being Destroyed*

It will comfort you so much to remember that your beloved is not confined to that body you see on the bed. If you can hold onto this understanding, *you will be able to bring something rare and beautiful into his room with you: acceptance and peace.*

Though you may be shaken to the very core by the changes in his body, you will remind yourself again and again that your beloved is embarking on a perfectly safe and pleasurable journey. He is not sailing off the edge of the Earth. You will not be afraid for him in the slightest, nor will you be undone by grief.

THE TITANIC OR THE CONCORDE?

Your beloved is not going down with the ship. Your beloved is traveling first class on the *Concorde,* to the destination of his dreams. Remember Benjamin Franklin's marvelous words:

> *Our friend and we are invited abroad on a party of pleasure which is to last forever. His chair was ready first, and he is gone before us. We could not all conveniently start together; and why should you and I be grieved at this, since we are soon to follow, and know where to find him?*

Why should you be grieved? It's a party of *pleasure*. It's a luxury cruise. You are invited, too. You will join him one day. The depth and strength of your love, which you can easily measure by feeling the pain you're in right now, guarantee your reunion. This is not a metaphor. This is the truth.

Tool: *The Body Is the Wrapping Paper, The Beloved Is the Gift*

What do you see when you look at your beloved? You see the package the beloved is wrapped in. You see the apartment the beloved lives in. You see the car the beloved was using to get around town. You do *not* see the beloved.

You see the complex package (fluids, minerals, living cells of all kinds) that for all *practical* purposes (hugging, laughing, eating, speaking) have been surrounding and serving the beloved all these years. You see the form the beloved has been using to share your life for a little while. You do *not* see the beloved. You see the camouflage the beloved has been wearing, but you cannot see the shape of the beloved as he or she really is. The essential beloved is invisible to the eye.

LANGUAGE AND LOVE

One of the hardest things to bear when someone we love approaches death is the breach in communication that opens up. Since the connection we know best is often mediated by language, it can be excruciating when language no longer serves, when responses cannot be had, when even the basic "I love you" cannot be exchanged.

This is the time to remember how inadequate words are to convey your love. The *big* love, not mere affection, but deep connections like the one you have with your beloved cannot even be suggested, much less conveyed, by mere words. You already know this, too.

I remember the first time I felt the full power of this nonverbal connection. Hedley was just five weeks old, sleeping and eating 'round the clock: lights on, nobody home, just normal newborn stuff. This particular evening I picked her up to nurse her even though she was sound asleep. It was Mother's Day and though I usually let sleeping babies lie, this time I was so filled with gratitude for her that I felt I'd burst if I didn't release some of it.

Our room was dark except for the wedge of light that fell across my bed from the slightly open door. I sat on the bed and held her to me. She drank and drank without appearing to wake up at all. And then, as I rested her little body on my lap and stared with wonder at her amazing little face, she opened her eyes, paused a moment and then fully and consciously *smiled* at me.

She was all there, exactly as she is now, eight years later. Her wide eyes sparkled with intelligence, recognition and love. No, I wasn't imagining it. She had been awake before, of course. But she had never been *present* and now she was. We recognized one another, we knew each other all over again without a word. The exchange was so full, subtle and complex. I was flooded with joy without a single word.

Moreover, the few words I've used to try to share the moment with you don't begin to do the job. And I've tried hard. It's close but no cigar. You do know what I mean, though, don't you? Because you've had a love so full, a connection so deep, that you wouldn't dream of trying to drape language over it.

Words often obscure what they're meant to express. It's like tossing a sheet over Michelangelo's *David*. You can make out the general shape of the masterpiece, but if you want really to experience it, you have to strip away the sheet and just be quiet, and look and feel.

Tool: *Memory Is a Silent Movie That Never Ends*

If the beloved is your parent or child, your husband, wife or life partner, then you have a treasure chest filled with memories of the many hours you spent together. Think of these memories, the record of your life with your beloved, as being stored on many videotapes—pictures only, though, plus the theme music that ran through those years and will always be linked in your heart to those times, no words.

You will be able to comfort yourself later by playing as many of these tapes as you like, as often as you like. Nothing will erase them. And *if* you can hold onto the knowledge that your beloved has been relocated, not destroyed, you will rejoice to play those tapes. It's a big "if," though, isn't it? How can you imagine your beloved as both intact and intangible, present and missing at the same time? Here are some ways to understand this.

What if the room you are sitting in now were demolished? If the floors, the ceiling, the walls and all the furniture were suddenly to disappear, what would remain? The space itself would still be there, wouldn't it? It's just that you wouldn't be able to identify its previous boundaries. The limiting structures would be gone. But the *space* itself would be *where* it always was. And it would be unchanged. It would be exactly *what* it always was as well. Are you with me? Here's another analogy.

What if you kept a bottle of water beside you at the beach? In the evening, rather than carry home what's left in the bottle, you walk down to the shore, upend the bottle and add your drinking water to the sea. Did your water cease to exist? Of course not. Now it's everywhere the sea is. Could you get that very same water back into your bottle? Of course not. It's been dispersed into the vastness of the sea.

It is not limited by the container anymore. In that sense only, it is gone.

That's the problem in a nutshell when someone we've loved and have been living with dies. We cannot find the familiar form, so we think that the content has been obliterated, too—such a natural error and such a painful one.

ANOTHER ANALOGY

What happens when you go to the movies? You see images of actors and actresses moving about on a big flat screen. You might tell a friend afterward, "I saw Dustin Hoffman in *Tootsie*. I saw Meryl Streep in *The Bridges of Madison County*." Did you really? No. You saw their images, made of light and shadow, caught on a strip of celluloid and projected on a screen. But you say you saw *them*.

It's a kind of shorthand. Everybody knows what you mean, though. You mean you saw an image of an actor playing a role. And you enjoyed the actor *in that role*. But if you ran into Dustin Hoffman at the supermarket, you might say, "Wow, you were terrific in *Tootsie*!" You wouldn't say, "So, how did things work out between you and your girlfriend's father?" And if you ran into Meryl Streep, you wouldn't scold her for betraying her husband.

You remain aware of the distinction between the actor and the role, don't you? If you are a fan of Hoffman or Streep—or both—you might try to see any movie they were in. And though you might become engrossed in the story, you would still remain aware that you're watching Streep or Hoffman create another brilliant illusion: accents, mannerisms, costumes and all.

The essence, the individuality of the actor, remain intact, unmistakable and unique. Only roles change. But you'd know that actor anywhere, right? Now let's return to your beloved, who's going to be dying soon.

What Is the Beloved?

Our bodies are lent us, as Ben Franklin says. *We* are permanent, and *they* are not. We endure, they disintegrate. That's all there is to it. What drew you to the beloved in the first place? Even though the physical form was pleasing to you, no doubt, it was that ***unique spirit,*** the dear being who animated the physical form, who caught your heart. It was the sparkle, the laughter and the seriousness, too, the precise arrangement of pleasing elements, blended with just the right amount of challenge, difficulty and lack, to keep you interested and growing. Your love is based on these durable qualities and not on the ever-changing physical form, which was heading into oblivion from the moment you two met.

Just the Love

What is your relationship made of? Just the love. What has endured all the changes in each of you over the years? Must be the love. When the beloved's body has been left behind, what will become of your love? Will it disintegrate when the body does? Or will your devotion to the beloved deepen and grow?

Au Revoir and Bon Voyage

What if you were standing on the dock watching a sleek magnificent cruise ship gradually ease back from the pier? What if your beloved were waving from the deck? What if you had shared as many last hugs as possible in the state-room? What if you had exchanged "I love you" again and again, until you both knew you didn't need to say it anymore? Until you both knew the love went way beyond little words and always would?

Now the physical separation is almost complete. You can only wave from the pier. No more hugs now. No more words. The figure of your beloved grows tiny and indistinct. You cannot be sure it is he anymore. You cannot make out his face. The tugs nudge his ship out into the river and swing the prow downstream toward the sea. Now you cannot even see it anymore. You slowly walk away toward your car. Quiet tears. Heavy heart.

Is this a nonevent? Of course not. It is one of the most moving and important moments of your life. You and he have had so much fun together—have shared so many years of life, have counted on each other for everything. There is not another person who is anything like him. How could there be?

But is the sensation you're having right now sadness or is it grief? What's the difference, you ask? Try these questions:

1. *Can anything make you smile or laugh?*   Yes   No

2. *Can you talk to someone about how you feel?*   Yes   No

3. *Will you? Do you?*   Yes   No

4. *Are you crying readily off and on?*   Yes   No

5. *Does your food taste all right?*   Yes   No

6. *Does everything seem awfully difficult?*   Yes   No

7. *Are you having trouble getting to sleep?*   Yes   No

8. *Are you having trouble waking up?*   Yes   No

9. *Does everything feel terribly flat?*   Yes   No

10. *Has everyone let you down?*   Yes   No

If you circled "Yes" for the most part on the first five questions and "No" mostly on the second five, then let's call what you are going through sadness, not grief.

Notice that, in any case, your thoughts return to your loved one again and again. If you are in grief, then every time you think of him, it will be painful. When the loss is new, you will be in that pain-filled condition all the time.

Grief makes it very hard to think clearly or at all. If you *were* able to think, though, and I asked you what belief was at the root of your agony, you would find that it is the Annihilation Premise one more time. You believe your beloved *is no more*. And as we have said again and again, if that *were* the case, no amount of grief could ever be sufficient. I grieved over my mother's death for eleven years because I thought she was obliterated. Once I knew that was not the case, my grief shifted to sadness.

MUST YOU GRIEVE?

Isn't it important to grieve? Isn't the grief process necessary in order to integrate the loss and move on? I don't think so at all. Grief is not logical, not appropriate, not necessary, and in my view, not at all beneficial. But sadness makes all kinds of sense. It's the time we need and want to honor the beloved, to let our thoughts go to the beloved whenever they will. And to cry. Sadness includes the possibility of talking about the beloved with a friend. It includes the possibility of an evening of dinner and the movies. It includes the possibility of making fun of your own condition (as Joan did when she described herself as "beating a dead horse"). It includes the occasional good deep laugh—and cry.

Sadness does not have to be painful. It can be sacred and deep and rich and even quite delicious. Why try to push it away? So much of the time we live on the surface of our being. But now we are deep inside. The textures of life are different. Nothing seems routine right now. The beloved is present in you and *as* you all the time. *If* you didn't feel that it should have been some other way, *if* you didn't think the beloved was annihilated when his body went, you'd be savoring the time you're spending thinking about him now. And it wouldn't be painful at all. It's just habit that makes us experience it that way.

Tool: *It's Moving Day*

Your dying friend is moving out of her apartment. She has already found a new place—a much nicer one—and so she isn't much interested in the old one anymore. What you see when you come over to help with packing is that the place is a mess. There are old newspapers and boxes everywhere, and nothing looks anything like the neat lovely little home she once had.

Moreover, the heat isn't working, the electricity is out, you're packing by candlelight and the hot water is off as well. You don't wonder that she wants to move out. If anything, you wish she hadn't waited quite so long to give up the old place.

You will notice that your friend is more than a little disoriented. This is so understandable and natural. After all, she is neither here nor there. She may drift from room to room, forgetting what she came in to the kitchen to do, standing dazed and lost in the middle of what once was her living room. And no wonder she's confused: it doesn't look anything like her living room anymore.

She may be going about her final tasks a little slowly, spacing out from time to time, literally absentminded. You may become irritated and impatient with the process. You may find yourself wishing she would just get it over with.

You may have something else you'd rather be doing even though you truly love your friend. And thoughts like that may make you think ill of yourself or feel guilty. Notice this: It's called adding insult to injury and we do it to ourselves mercilessly. Stop.

The whole process is very unnerving—you do want to be with her and help her with this move, but on the other hand, you'd give anything to be someplace else right now. And how exactly can you help her? You really don't have a clue.

What's Your Role?

The most important thing that you can do is remember:

Remember that your friend is not her body. And remember that the passage out of the body is blissful, not painful. Have no fear for her.

Remember that you are certain to undergo the same transition. Have no pity for her.

Remember that she is doing this in her own perfect way. If she has always been restless, angry or grumpy, she is likely to be so now. Individual style is as much a part of death as it is of life. Deathbed transformations are relatively rare in my experience.

Remember that you are there to *be with,* not to *do for.* Of course, if your friend is not receiving adequate pain relief, or if her sheets need changing or her mouth is dry, you will want to see that these matters are attended to. But otherwise, you are there to bear witness to your love for your friend and to bring her peace.

It's an Inside Job

Remember that the changes going on in your friend's body are being experienced by her from the *inside.* They are not anything like what they look like to you. She and her body have begun to part company. Remember the analogy of moving day. She is not fully at home in her body anymore. Don't try to pull her back or engage her unnecessarily in your concerns. Remember that her drifting in and out of consciousness is natural, and provides a respite from the discomfort her body might otherwise subject her to. Try to relax with this. She is still who she always was. She's just leaving town, that's all. Her perfect unique spirit remains intact. And so does her love for you.

SUGGESTIONS FOR HOSPITAL OR HOSPICE VISITS

If this is your first time seeing a beloved family member or friend dying, you may find some of the following suggestions helpful. These are the things I wish someone had told me in those last four days at my mother's side.

SLOW DOWN

Time gets very erratic when someone you love is dying. You may notice that it drags on and on when you're sitting by the bedside, that it rushes past when you're taking a break and that it stops altogether with each bit of "bad news" the doctors bring.

This is entirely normal, but it does contribute to the disorientation, the sense of strangeness you no doubt feel. It's as if you have dropped into a looking-glass world, where everything is both familiar and unreal, peculiar.

You may also notice that it's hard to leave home for the hospital "on time." Once you do get out the door, you may feel "behind schedule" and try to speed up the trip. So you arrive at the hospital breathless, apologetic, upset. This im-

mediately puts you out of sync with the much slower and
quieter energy of your beloved, who hasn't rushed anywhere
in days.

Stop in the restroom before you go upstairs. Wash your
hands, run a wet paper towel over your face, slow down.
Then go sit for a few moments at least in the hospital chapel.
And never mind if it's Catholic and you're Jewish or Protes-
tant or none of these. Even if you never liked God in the first
place, or are very angry with God right now, or don't know
anyone who answers to that name, the chapel is there for
you.

Collect yourself. Feel the peace in the room. Breathe
deeply and slowly. Gather in the comfort of God's love,
which is always surrounding your beloved and you. Then remind yourself that the beloved is not the stricken body in the
bed. Remind yourself that the form is not the content. The
beloved is simply leaving town, that's all. *Now* you're ready
to go upstairs.

CONNECT

Even if your beloved is not apparently conscious, you can
still connect. Sit beside the bed, hold a hand and silently say
the things you would say if the beloved were awake. If there
are things you regret having said or done, you can express
them now. If you think it's too late to apologize, you're
wrong. You can cover a lot of ground right here and now.
Your beloved is in dialogue with you in a subtle fashion. You
are not alone in the room.

And don't beat yourself up. We are all learning, all doing
the best we can manage at the time. Your beloved has a few
flaws, too, though you may feel uneasy remembering them
now. Give yourself permission to forgive the beloved, too.

Your forgiveness is a gift and a necessity for both of you. Don't withhold it now.

You can throw out cold leftovers like anger and regret later on. Just hear the voice of the beloved saying, "I wish I hadn't done it that way. You are precious to me. I made an awful mistake." And hear yourself respond with trust and forgiveness. Don't hold out if the beloved never said these words directly to you. You will torment yourself needlessly if you don't forgive.

Imagine that the beloved is sitting inside that luxury jet as it eases back from the gate. You are watching as the plane slowly taxis toward the takeoff runway. Your connection to the beloved is intact, but much more subtle and refined than it previously was. No, you can't hug each other or go out for dinner. But you are joined at the heart and always will be.

If you plan to spend some time in the room, give yourself permission to read or write, to listen to music or to pray. If you occupy your mind in these ways, you are less likely to get caught in the painful trap of cataloguing your beloved's physical decline, or speculating about how much time remains, or whether there is hope for some "better" outcome. Physical death is the one *possible* outcome for the body. The great mystery is whether it will come sooner or later. You are not the master of that moment; the beloved is.

Revisit some of the best memories you have. This is one time when it's really helpful to use the present moment, the only moment, to celebrate the past. You have had a rich and wonderful relationship, which is moving into a new stage now. Your connection to the beloved is intact, now and always. It is becoming more subtle, that's all.

It is being refined like the watery sap of a maple tree,

boiled down into something very concentrated and sweet. You will be able to mix that unmistakable sweetness into every moment of your future life. You will be able to taste it easily. You are loved.

A NOTE TO CLERGY

W HAT COULD BE MORE challenging than the death
of a member of your community? Yours is the
hard job of bringing comfort and support to the
pained survivors. If the death was sudden and unanticipated,
they will feel shock and disbelief as well. If you have never
lost someone yourself, you may feel quite incapable of approaching the mourner with any confidence.

The suffering person has slid into a pit of grief. How can
you help? Figuratively speaking, there are only two possibilities. You can either jump into the pit yourself, or you can
stay where you are, lower a rope, and pull the suffering person out. Let's look at both approaches.

JUMPING INTO THE PIT

This is the move that feels compassionate and loving. It often
looks like the right way to go. But is it really? Agreeing with
the mourner that this death is tragic, unwarranted, untimely,
and unfair is certainly the path of least resistance. It may
even be what the mourner expects, or wants. But is this approach consistent with what you really believe?

Do you represent a God who makes mistakes? Do you
speak for a God who can't quite get everything under control? Do you represent a God who fails to love everyone

equally? In other words, is your Lord omniscient, omnipotent and unimaginably loving?

If you believe this, then there *is* no tragedy happening here. There is no other way it *should* have gone. And there is a gift of tremendous love concealed in this event. It is from God, expressly for your mourner. It will be revealed over time. Your job as clergy is to keep the attention of your mourner focused on this level, even though the pain of loss is severe, even though the pit of grief seems appropriate, reasonable and safe, both to the mourner and to you.

LOWERING THE ROPE

The only rope you have is the truth. Death must come to every body. *And* there is no death. These naked facts may strike you as too much for the mourner to absorb. Not so. Now as never before, there is a pressing need to make sense out of this death and every death. An extraordinary receptivity arises from the grief. The mourner is desperate to understand and bear what has happened. It's lonely, dark and miserable in that grief pit.

Sounds too easy? What's the hitch? It's this: *You* have to have a *very* firm hold on that rope. You can't just drop the rope into the pit and expect the mourner to be able to climb out. Your faith, in other words, is the key factor here. You'll need a strong conviction of God's unerring goodness. You'll need the courage of that conviction, too.

PULLING THE MOURNER OUT

The Annihilation Premise, as we have called it, is what most people believe. You as clergy, of whatever faith tradition, know that the holy human spirit endures beyond the body's death. Pulling the mourner out of that pit depends on your ability to remind (or persuade) the mourner that the beloved is just out of town.

Once that concept is in place, your mourner is within reach. Now you can extend your hand, which holds all the tools of compassion, God's compassion and yours, untainted by pity, undiluted by fear.

The hardest part, the tough love part of your job, must be done first. If "why me, why this, why now?" is where your mourner is stuck, you have to be able to say, gently but clearly, "why not?" And if you cannot be heard at first, you must persist until you *are* heard. Self-pity, which permeates those questions, is such a dreary, useless and unnerving frame of mind. Many of my clergy friends don't know how to handle it. Tackling it head-on, directly, firmly and with love, works best.

If you can find a way to stir in some humor, like reminding the widow or widower that this parting was mentioned in the marriage ceremony, the truth may be easier to hear. Know, however, that even if it's not easy to hear, everyone recognizes the truth when it's spoken:

- this separation had to come.

- there is no basis for complaint.

- the separation is temporary.

- the bond of love endures.

The death of someone in your community is a wonderful opportunity to see how alive and robust your own faith is. If you have not yet been through the death of someone very close, it's hard to know how sturdy your belief structure is. Would it support *you* under the weight of a loss like the one your mourner has sustained? How would *you* react to hearing the things you want to say to the mourner? Do you sound sincere? *Are* you?

These questions cut so close to the bone both personally and professionally that they are sometimes difficult for ordained clergy to embrace. The biggest barrier is the notion that you are supposed to have a permanent handle on this issue. If you know you are shaky in this critical area, you might choose to avoid rather than to explore it. If you are a human being, this is natural.

Working for a decade in AIDS service, I have had conversations with hundreds and hundreds of people confronting death without any belief system to temper their grief or allay their fear. In the beginning, I was abashed by all the suffering. I felt that I had no right to say that death is, well, not as final as all that, and also not something there is any way around. I was reluctant to offend, and had no practice at dancing lightly with these truths. I was terribly serious and earnest all the time, and that alone was probably enough to nullify any good I might have done.

I was terribly afraid of making a fool of myself, as who is not? "Oh, my goodness, I might not say the right thing. I might make this suffering person worse, not better. Well, if I say nothing, they stay the same, and if I annoy them, their anger will be a nice respite from the pain. Let me try."

Honestly, even with no gifts to offer, just the fact of coming forward with *something* will convey the love.

The best response that you can offer is the one you've never made before. Reinvent your understanding of the nature of death every time you are called on to use it. To be spontaneous every time, you will have to believe what you are saying. It is your conviction that will help the mourner, more than any specific words.

For a Christian, the belief that Christ overcame death is absolutely central. Nonetheless, it's undeniably hard to apply that knowledge to an unanticipated death in one's own life. Maybe that's why the celebration of Easter has to be a yearly event. We all need to see this again and again. Even then, we get it and forget it continuously. Christ's contemporary disciples had a hard time with this one, too.

So don't beat yourself up. It's unlikely that any of your colleagues has it all mastered either. Pull the issue toward you boldly, then. There is so much to gain. You will be more sure of yourself after every experience. Relax. Remember that God isn't finished with you yet.

One suggestion is not to use any scriptural references in your first conversation with the mourner. And it's fine to refer to an event in the Bible. But tell the story, or cite the example, in your own words, using your most ordinary everyday vocabulary. Although being clergy is what got you connected with the mourner, being as natural as any layperson is what will help you get through right now, especially if the mourner is a contemporary.

After "why me, why this, why now?" is addressed, the rest is listening.